A Short Introduction to the Rights of Nature

Ecem Çoban Bilici

A Short Introduction to the Rights of Nature

A Discourse on Its Philosophy and Recognition in International Law

PETER LANG

Berlin · Bruxelles · Chennai · Lausanne · New York · Oxford

Bibliographic information published by the Deutsche Nationalbibliothek.
The German National Library lists this publication in the German National Bibliography; detailed bibliographic data is available on the Internet at http://dnb.d-nb.de.

A catalogue record for this book is available from the British Library.

Library of Congress Control Number: 2026934808

Cover design by Peter Lang Group AG

ISBN 978-3-631-93913-0 (Print)
ISBN 978-3-631-93916-1 (ePDF)
ISBN 978-3-631-93917-8 (ePUB)
DOI 10.3726/b22986

Published by Peter Lang GmbH, Berlin (Germany)

info@peterlang.com

www.peterlang.com

Contact for General Product Safety Regulation (GPSR): gpsr@peterlang.com

To Mavi,
a dream more beautiful than I ever dared to imagine.

Table of Contents

Preface

This work, originally written as my master's thesis in Law (LLM) at Pompeu Fabra University, Barcelona in 2018, emerges at a critical juncture when Earth's living systems face unprecedented ecological challenges. From climate change to biodiversity loss, with devastating impacts on all forms of life, the fundamental inadequacy of traditional environmental protection frameworks becomes increasingly apparent. This book aims to serve as an introductory guide to an emerging and transformative legal concept: the Rights of Nature.

The inquiry that led to this work began with a fundamental question: Why do existing environmental protection mechanisms consistently fail to prevent ecological degradation? The answer lies not in the mechanisms themselves but in their philosophical foundations. Current legal systems, built upon centuries of anthropocentric thought, remain fundamentally incapable of addressing ecological challenges that require recognition of nature's intrinsic value and inherent rights.

This book examines the philosophical evolution and practical implementation of nature's rights across three interconnected dimensions. First, it traces the historical development of human–nature relationships, revealing how religious doctrines, philosophical traditions, and economic systems have reinforced the subordination of nature. Second, it explores the theoretical foundations of nature's rights, integrating classical philosophical critique with contemporary environmental ethics. Finally, and significantly, it provides a comprehensive analysis of how the rights of nature can be recognised and protected within international law. This international legal dimension examines both existing mechanisms and emerging frameworks, while addressing crucial questions of implementation, enforcement, and the role of international institutions in protecting nature's inherent rights. This multi-layered analysis aims to demonstrate how international law can evolve to better recognise and protect the rights of all natural entities across jurisdictional boundaries.

While comprehensive in scope, this work is intended as an accessible introduction to the rights of nature movement. It aims to bridge the gap between theoretical discourse and practical implementation, illuminating pathways for recognising and protecting the inherent rights of all natural entities. The analysis draws upon diverse sources – from ancient philosophical texts to contemporary court decisions – to demonstrate how recognition of nature's rights represents not merely an incremental improvement in environmental protection but a fundamental transformation in the relationship between human and non-human nature.

The urgency of this transformation cannot be overstated. As Earth's life-supporting systems face accelerating deterioration, the need for fundamental reconceptualisation of environmental protection becomes increasingly apparent. The rights of nature movement offers pathways toward more effective ecological preservation – pathways that this book seeks to illuminate.

I am deeply grateful to Pompeu Fabra University Faculty of Law for providing an enriching academic environment during my LL.M. studies. I would also like to express my gratitude to Dr Serkan Köybaşı for sharing his valuable insights on this manuscript.

This book emerges from the recognition that human–nature relationships require fundamental transformation – not merely for the survival of individual species but for the flourishing of Earth's entire living system. It is offered as both analysis and invitation: an analysis of how to better protect Earth's intricate web of life, and an invitation to imagine and implement legal frameworks that recognise and protect the inherent rights of all natural entities.

Ecem ÇOBAN BİLİCİ
İstanbul, 2024

The Evolution of Environmental Protection: An Introduction

The relationship between humanity and nature has undergone profound transformations throughout history. In antiquity, nature held a sacred status across diverse civilisations, embedded within religious cosmologies and cultural frameworks that afforded it a degree of protection, albeit insufficient to prevent anthropogenic environmental degradation. Even in these early periods, human activities – from the expansion of agriculture to urbanisation and warfare – exerted considerable pressure on natural systems, though at a scale incomparable to contemporary environmental challenges. This relatively stable paradigm experienced a fundamental shift with the emergence of rationalist philosophical movements and the expansion of anthropocentric religious interpretations that positioned humanity as nature's designated steward. This transformation effectively dissolved the notion of nature's inherent sanctity, fundamentally altering the human–nature relationship into what can be characterised as an increasingly asymmetrical interaction.

The formal recognition that ecosystems, water bodies, and atmospheric systems might warrant legal protection emerged belatedly in the late nineteenth century, marking a crucial transition in environmental consciousness.[1] This development coincided with advancing scientific understanding and industrial expansion, leading to the gradual evolution of environmental law. The post-World War II period marked a pivotal moment in this progression,

1 Tarlock, A. D. (2009). History of environmental law. In A. D. Tarlock & J. C. Dembach (Eds.), *Environmental laws and their enforcement* (Vol. 1, pp. 41–65). Encyclopedia of Life Support Systems.

as the vulnerability of the biosphere to human-induced deterioration gained widespread acknowledgement. The 1960s witnessed the crystallisation of these concerns into concrete legal frameworks, with developed nations implementing various environmental protection measures.[2] This period also saw the emergence of numerous non-governmental institutions and the development of diverse legal instruments, elevating environmental law from a purely domestic concern to an integral component of international legal discourse. By the 1970s, environmental law had established itself as an interdisciplinary field with international scope, characterised by the proliferation of institutions and multilateral agreements aimed at environmental preservation. However, despite this extensive legal and institutional evolution, the fundamental ecological crisis persists, suggesting the inadequacy of conventional approaches to environmental protection.

This historical progression reveals a crucial insight: while environmental law has evolved considerably in both scope and sophistication, it remains fundamentally rooted in the same anthropocentric paradigm that has historically characterised human–nature relations. The persistence and intensification of environmental degradation, despite increasingly comprehensive legal frameworks, suggests that the crisis we face today transcends conventional regulatory approaches. To fully comprehend the magnitude of our current ecological predicament and the inadequacy of existing legal responses, it is essential to examine the unprecedented scale and complexity of contemporary environmental challenges, particularly as they manifest in the current ecological crisis.

1.1 The Contemporary Ecological Crisis: Beyond Anthropogenic Impact

Earth's complex systems operate within a delicate equilibrium that, while accommodating natural fluctuations and periodic disruptions, maintains a remarkable capacity for self-regulation and restoration.[3] This intrinsic resilience, however, faces unprecedented challenges in the contemporary era. As

---

[2] Pūraitė, A. (2012). Origins of environmental regulation. *Jurisprudencija, 19*(2), 657–674.

[3] Schwartzman, D. (1999). *Life, temperature, and the earth: The self-organizing biosphere* (p. 191). Columbia University Press.

Kricher notably observes, “Never in the 4.5 billion-year history of Earth has but one species had such an inordinate influence on all others, and in such a short span of time”.[4] This observation is now substantiated by extensive scientific evidence: contemporary research demonstrates an overwhelming consensus regarding anthropogenic climate change and its cascading effects on global ecological systems.[5]

The manifestations of this unprecedented disruption are both profound and multifaceted. Global climate change triggers a complex chain of environmental responses: the accelerated melting of polar ice sheets contributes to rising sea levels, threatening coastal ecosystems and human settlements alike. Marine systems face particular vulnerability, with oceanic warming leading to decreased oxygen levels and increased acidification, fundamentally altering marine ecosystems and threatening biodiversity.[6] These transformations extend beyond isolated environmental impacts, creating interconnected crises that challenge both ecological and social stability.

The ramifications of these environmental alterations extend into critical domains of human security and ecological integrity. Water scarcity, food insecurity, and forced migration emerge as inevitable consequences, potentially catalysing social and political instability. The intensification of extreme weather events, coupled with the proliferation of vector-borne diseases and the escalation of forest fires, creates a self-reinforcing cycle of environmental degradation. This cycle is further exacerbated by increasing carbon dioxide concentrations, creating a feedback loop that threatens both human populations and ecological systems. The scope and severity of these impacts compel even traditional advocates of anthropocentric approaches to acknowledge the fundamental inadequacy of current legal and regulatory frameworks in addressing these unprecedented challenges.

---

4 Kricher, J. (2009). *The balance of nature: Ecology's enduring myth* (p. 4). Princeton University Press.

5 Cook, J. et al. (2013). Quantifying the consensus on anthropogenic global warming in the scientific literature. *Environmental Research Letters, 8*(2), 024024.

6 Welch, C. (2018, January 4). Climate change is suffocating large parts of the ocean. *National Geographic*. https://news.nationalgeographic.com/2018/01/climate-change-suffocating-low-oxygen-zones-ocean/.

1.2 From Conservation to Rights: The Journey of Environmental Law

The emergence of environmental regulations marked a significant, albeit instrumentalist, response to mounting ecological challenges. As anthropogenic impacts – from global warming to resource depletion and widespread pollution – became increasingly evident, legal frameworks evolved to address these concerns. However, this evolution, while representing a notable advancement in environmental protection, remained fundamentally anchored in anthropocentric presumptions. These early environmental regulations, despite their protective intent, perpetuated the conceptualisation of nature as an object of human utility rather than a subject of inherent rights.

The philosophical underpinnings of environmental law reveal its inherent limitations. Environmental protection, as traditionally conceived, operates primarily through the lens of intergenerational human interests and sustainable resource management. This approach manifests in regulatory frameworks designed to "limit ecological impacts that threaten public health and biodiversity",[7] yet notably stops short of questioning the fundamental relationship between humanity and nature. The protection afforded to natural entities remains contingent upon their instrumental value to human societies – rivers are preserved for their utility in agriculture and drinking water, forests for their role in climate regulation and resource provision, and species for their contribution to biodiversity and potential human benefit.[8]

This anthropocentric orientation is particularly evident in the tripartite objectives that emerged from the environmental movement of the 1960s: pollution control for human health, conservation for future generations, and sustainable development for continued economic growth.[9] While these objectives represented significant progress in environmental protection, they fundamentally positioned environmental law as a balancing mechanism between human economic interests and resource sustainability. This framework, however sophisticated in its regulatory approach, proves increasingly

---

7 Lazarus, R. J. (2004). *The making of environmental law* (p. 1). University of Chicago Press.

8 Pūraitė, A. (2012). Origins of environmental regulation. *Jurisprudencija, 19*(2), 657–674.

9 Tarlock, A. D. (2009). History of environmental law. In A. D. Tarlock & J. C. Dembach (Eds.), *Environmental laws and their enforcement* (Vol. 1, pp. 41–65). Encyclopedia of Life Support Systems.

inadequate in addressing contemporary ecological challenges. The persistence and acceleration of environmental degradation, despite increasingly comprehensive legal protections, suggests that a more fundamental transformation in environmental jurisprudence is necessary – one that transcends the traditional conservationist paradigm and moves toward a rights-based conceptualisation of nature.

1.3 Shifting Perspectives in Nature–Human Relations

The underlying aetiology of the contemporary ecological crisis extends beyond mere regulatory inadequacies, residing deeply within the evolution of human self-conception and its relationship to the natural world. Despite the proliferation of environmental legislation since the 1970s, a fundamental transformation in humanity's orientation toward nature remains conspicuously absent. The anthropocentric positioning that emerged historically has not only persisted but has become increasingly entrenched, manifesting in a systematic denial of the fundamental interconnectedness between human and non-human entities within the ecological web.[10]

This hierarchical conceptualisation of human–nature relations finds its legitimation through various theological and philosophical constructs. Religious doctrines frequently position humanity as divinely appointed stewards of creation, while philosophical traditions emphasise human rationality and linguistic capability as markers of superiority. These legitimating frameworks have effectively sanctioned an increasingly exploitative relationship with the natural world, creating what environmental philosophers term the "differential imperative" – the selective emphasis on particular human capabilities as justification for ecological dominion.[11]

The persistence of this anthropocentric orientation represents more than mere philosophical positioning; it manifests in concrete approaches to environmental protection. The belated recognition of environmental degradation as a pressing concern emerged not from an acknowledgement of nature's

---

[10] Steiner, G. (2010). *Anthropocentrism and its discontents: The moral status of animals in the history of western philosophy* (p. 2). University of Pittsburgh Press.

[11] Rodman, J. (1980). Paradigm change in political science. *American Behavioral Scientist, 24*, 49–78.

intrinsic value, but rather from the growing awareness of environmental deterioration's adverse impacts on human welfare. This reactive rather than proactive stance highlights the deeply rooted nature of anthropocentric thinking in contemporary environmental consciousness.[12] The instrumental view of nature – as resource, as utility, as subject of human management – continues to dominate environmental discourse and policy, even as mounting evidence suggests the fundamental unsustainability of this paradigm.

This entrenched perspective now faces unprecedented challenges as the scale and scope of ecological degradation force a reconsideration of traditional human–nature relationships. The emergence of more nuanced understandings of ecological interconnectedness, coupled with growing recognition of the limitations of anthropocentric approaches, suggests the possibility – indeed, the necessity – of a fundamental shift in how humanity conceptualises its relationship with the natural world.[13]

1.4 The Emergence of Nature's Legal Personhood

The dominance of anthropocentric approaches in environmental law has increasingly faced substantive philosophical and practical challenges. As Tarlock notably observes, "Conservation (environmentalism) is getting us nowhere because it is incompatible with our Abrahamic concept of land. We abuse land because we regard it as a commodity belonging to us".[14] This critique has catalysed the development of alternative theoretical frameworks that fundamentally reconceptualise the human–nature relationship in legal and philosophical discourse.

These counter-narratives to anthropocentric dominance manifest in various theoretical orientations, ranging from eco-fascism to bio-centrism and ultimately culminating in ecocentric approaches. The ecocentric paradigm, particularly noteworthy for its comprehensive reformulation of

12 Eckersley, R. (1997). *Environmentalism and political theory: Toward an ecocentric approach* (p. 49). UCL Press.

13 Taylor, P. W. (2011). *Respect for nature: A theory of environmental ethics* (p. 258). Princeton University Press.

14 Tarlock, A. D. (2009). History of environmental law. In A. D. Tarlock & J. C. Dembach (Eds.), *Environmental laws and their enforcement* (Vol. 1, pp. 41–65). Encyclopedia of Life Support Systems.

environmental ethics, encompasses diverse theoretical strands including eco-feminism, social ecology, deep ecology, and eco-socialism. The various ecological philosophical approaches – from eco-feminism and social ecology to deep ecology and eco-socialism – despite their methodological and theoretical distinctions, converge on a fundamental premise: the recognition of nature's inherent rights. This recognition represents a radical departure from traditional legal frameworks, establishing nature as an autonomous legal entity with enforceable rights rather than merely an object of human management and protection.

The transition from theoretical framework to legal implementation marks a crucial evolution in environmental jurisprudence. Ecuador's 2008 constitutional recognition of the rights of nature represents a watershed moment in this progression, explicitly acknowledging ecosystems' "right to exist, persist, maintain and regenerate".[15] This precedent-setting development has inspired similar legal innovations across diverse jurisdictions, including India, Bolivia, and New Zealand, suggesting an emerging paradigm shift in environmental law. These developments reflect not merely incremental adjustments to existing legal frameworks but rather signal a fundamental reconceptualisation of nature's legal status.

The recognition of nature's legal personhood thus emerges as both a theoretical imperative and a practical necessity, bridging the gap between ecocentric philosophy and juridical practice. This evolution in legal thought provides the foundation for examining both the philosophical underpinnings of the rights of nature and their practical implementation in international legal frameworks, which will be explored in subsequent chapters.

1.5 Content Structure and Methodological Framework

This work constructs a systematic analytical framework for examining the rights of nature, integrating philosophical critique with emerging jurisprudential developments. The analysis proceeds from the premise that effective environmental protection requires fundamental reconceptualisation of

15 Milam, R. (2013). Rights of nature and our responsibilities as earth community. *The Rights of Nature*. https://www.therightsofnature.org.

human–nature relationships, moving beyond conventional anthropocentric frameworks toward recognition of nature's inherent rights.

The work's tripartite structure reflects the evolutionary progression of the rights of nature: from historical development through theoretical foundation to practical implementation. Chapter 1 establishes crucial historical context by examining the transformation of human–nature relationships, revealing how religious doctrines, philosophical traditions, and economic systems have reinforced anthropocentric dominion. This historical analysis demonstrates that current environmental challenges stem not merely from regulatory inadequacies but from fundamental misconceptions about humanity's relationship with nature.

Chapter 2 provides the theoretical foundation through systematic examination of anthropocentric worldviews, capitalist exploitation, and emerging ecocentric philosophy. The analysis integrates classical philosophical critiques with contemporary environmental ethics, demonstrating how traditional approaches – from utilitarianism through light green environmentalism – fail to address root causes of ecological degradation. This theoretical framework establishes the philosophical basis for recognising nature's intrinsic rights while anticipating implementation challenges.

Chapter 3 bridges philosophical foundations with practical implementation through analysis of emerging legal frameworks, from Ecuador's constitutional provisions through India's judicial innovations. This section examines both the potential and limitations of existing international mechanisms while developing frameworks for more effective protection. The analysis specifically addresses jurisdictional challenges, enforcement mechanisms, and the role of legal guardianship in protecting the rights of nature.

The methodology emphasises rigorous integration of theoretical analysis with practical case studies, enabling examination of both philosophical underpinnings and implementation challenges. This approach reveals how conventional environmental protection frameworks, constrained by anthropocentric assumptions, systematically fail to prevent ecological degradation.

Philosophical and Theoretical Foundations

2.1 Rethinking Nature's Place in Law: From Object to Subject

Contemporary environmental law rests upon three interconnected philosophical premises that have historically shaped humanity's relationship with nature.[16] These foundational concepts continue to influence legal, social, and economic approaches to environmental protection, while simultaneously facing increasing scrutiny in light of mounting ecological challenges.

The first and most pervasive of these premises is anthropocentrism – the conviction that humans occupy a position of fundamental superiority in the universal order. This deeply embedded worldview permeates virtually all economic, social, and environmental considerations, manifesting even in ostensibly protective environmental measures. Indeed, contemporary environmental protection frameworks frequently reflect this anthropocentric orientation, despite growing recognition of its limitations.

The second premise centres on the concept of natural ownership – the assertion that both living and non-living elements of the natural world exist primarily as human property, whether held individually or collectively. This notion of ownership has found various justifications throughout history: religious doctrines positioning nature as divinely granted for human use, philosophical arguments grounding human dominion in rational capacity, and legal frameworks codifying human authority over natural resources. This

16 Boyd, D. R. (2017). *The rights of nature: A legal revolution that could save the world* (p. xxii). ECW Press.

conceptual foundation provides the theoretical underpinning for utilitarian approaches to environmental management.

The third premise involves the perceived necessity of infinite economic growth in modern industrial society. This principle, fundamental to contemporary capitalism, profoundly shapes all economic, legal, and environmental relationships, establishing a paradigm where ecological considerations frequently yield to economic imperatives.

The emergence of modern environmental philosophy represents a significant challenge to these established paradigms. This evolving field has generated increasingly sophisticated theoretical frameworks that question long-held assumptions about human–nature relationships. Its development encompasses diverse approaches, from pragmatic reforms within existing systems to radical reconceptualisations of ecological relationships, enriching environmental discourse while suggesting multiple pathways toward addressing contemporary ecological challenges.

This chapter examines these theoretical foundations through several interconnected lenses, analysing their historical development, contemporary manifestations, and implications for environmental law. Both the philosophical underpinnings of current environmental legal frameworks and potential trajectories for their future evolution are aimed to be illuminated through this analysis.

2.1.1 The Anthropocentric Worldview: Origins and Manifestations

2.1.1.1 Historical Origins and Classical Philosophical Foundations

The concept of anthropocentrism stands as one of the most enduring and influential frameworks in human intellectual history. Etymologically derived from the ancient Greek roots "ánthrōpos"[17] and "-centric",[18] the term encapsulates the fundamental conviction that "human existence constitutes the most important and central fact in the universe".[19] This linguistic origin serves

[17] Anthropo-; word-forming element meaning "pertaining to man or human beings," from Greek ánthrōpos "man; human being" (including women). Anthropo-. (2017, June 7). In *Wiktionary*. https://en.wiktionary.org/wiki/anthropo-

[18] Having a specified object at the centre, or as the focus of attention. -Centric. (2017, July 27). In *Wiktionary*. https://en.wiktionary.org/wiki/-centric

[19] Anthropocentric. (n.d.). In *Cambridge Dictionary*. https://dictionary.cambridge.org/dictionary/english/anthropocentric

as more than etymology; it reflects an essential worldview that has shaped human understanding of their place in the cosmic order for millennia.

The historical trajectory of anthropocentric thought reveals its deep roots in pre-Socratic philosophy, where early Greek thinkers began formulating ideas about human distinctiveness. This formative period marked the initial systematic attempt to position humans as unique within the natural order, primarily through the emphasis on human rationality and consciousness.

Anthropocentrism, in its most thorough definition, represents "a viewpoint or theory that places human beings at the center of something, giving preference to human beings above all other considerations".[20] This philosophical stance transcends basic self-interest, embodying instead a sophisticated theoretical structure that has decisively influenced human civilisation's relationship with the natural world. The persistence and pervasiveness of this worldview is remarkable, as it has been "built up and reinforced over thousands of years of scholarship, predicated on the idea that humanity is fundamentally different from the rest of the natural world".[21]

However, this etymological and conceptual basis warrants rigorous examination. The emergence of this human-centred paradigm coincided with humanity's increasing technological capability to modify their environment, suggesting a potential correlation between power over nature and the philosophical justification of such dominion.

The philosophical implications of anthropocentric thought extend beyond human primacy. They establish a systematic construct for moral reasoning, epistemological understanding, and ontological positioning of humanity within the broader universe. The impact of this system lies not only in its theoretical underpinnings but in its practical consequences for human decision-making and ethical considerations.

Contemporary philosophical discourse has begun to undertake a systematic reassessment of the historical development of anthropocentric thought, particularly in light of mounting environmental challenges. This analysis has led scholars to question whether traditional anthropocentric approaches can

---

20 Anthropocentrism. (n.d.). In *Wiktionary*. https://en.wiktionary.org/wiki/anthropocentrism#English

21 Gillespie, A. (2014). *International environmental law, policy, and ethics* (p. 145). Oxford University Press.

adequately address current ecological crises. The philosopher Mary Midgley provides an incisive analysis of this worldview's scope and character:

Here people have seen themselves as placed, not just at the relative centre of a particular life, but at the absolute, objective centre of everything. The centrality of MAN (sic) has been pretty steadily conceived, both in the West and in many other traditions, not as an illusion of perspective imposed by our starting-point, but as an objective fact, and indeed an essential fact, about the whole universe.[22]

This transformation of anthropocentrism from philosophical position to presumed natural order illustrates how deeply embedded this outlook became in human thought systems. The reification of human centrality has shaped not only philosophical discourse but has defined legal, political, and social institutions, establishing a model that shapes modern environmental policy and ethics.

The persistence of these classical philosophical principles in contemporary thought demonstrates the enduring influence of early anthropocentric worldviews. However, the philosophical conceptualisation of human supremacy found its most powerful and enduring expression through religious doctrines. Religious traditions, particularly the Abrahamic faiths, played a pivotal role in sanctifying and institutionalising anthropocentric ideas, transforming philosophical postulations into divine mandates. This theological dimension of anthropocentrism would prove crucial in shaping humanity's relationship with nature for millennia to come.

2.1.1.2 Religious Doctrines and Nature's Subordination

The institutionalisation of anthropocentric thought reached its zenith through religious doctrine, particularly within the Abrahamic traditions. The theological endorsement of human supremacy in Christianity and Judaism established an enduring ideological structure that would profoundly shape humanity's relationship with nature. This religious legitimisation of anthropocentrism manifests most explicitly in the foundational texts of these traditions, notably in Genesis 1:28:

---

[22] Midgley, M. (1994). The end of anthropocentricism? In R. Attfield (Ed.), *Philosophy and the natural environment* (p. 104). Cambridge University Press.

> Then God blessed Noah and his sons, saying to them, "Be fruitful and increase in number and fill the earth. The fear and dread of you will fall on all the beasts of the earth, and on all the birds in the sky, on every creature that moves along the ground, and on all the fish in the sea; they are given into your hands. Everything that lives and moves about will be food for you. Just as I gave you the green plants, I now give you everything."[23]

It is crucial to note that these religious understandings of human dominion evolved within specific historical and social contexts. The reading of such texts has varied substantially across different periods and communities, ranging from concepts of absolute dominion to more nuanced ideas of stewardship and responsibility. This divine proclamation, interpreted as a "divine charge for absolute human sovereignty".[24] transformed philosophical anthropocentrism into sacred mandate, though its understanding has evolved across different historical periods and theological traditions.

The medieval period marked a critical juncture where religious doctrine merged with classical philosophical thought. This synthesis produced a sophisticated theological-philosophical system that would shape Western environmental attitudes for centuries. The scholastic tradition, particularly through figures like Thomas Aquinas (1225–1274), systematically integrated Aristotelian natural philosophy with Christian doctrine to create a comprehensive justification for human supremacy over nature. Thomas Aquinas, whose synthesis of Aristotelian philosophy and Christian theology proved influential, systematically developed the doctrine of human exceptionalism. While advancing the principle of human rational uniqueness, Aquinas explicitly rejected any intrinsic value in non-human nature, reinforcing the division between intellectual and physical realms.[25] His definitive statement on this matter reveals the depth of this hierarchical worldview:

> Dumb animals and plants are devoid of the life of reason whereby to set themselves in motion; they are moved, as it were by another, by a kind of natural impulse, a sign of which is that they are naturally enslaved and accommodated to the uses of others.[26]

---

23 The Holy Bible: New International Version. (2011). Genesis 1:28. Zondervan.

24 Moore, B. L. (2017). *Ecological literature and the critique of anthropocentrism* (p. 7). Palgrave Macmillan.

25 Gillespie, A. (2014). *International environmental law, policy, and ethics* (p. 6). Oxford University Press.

26 Aquinas, T. (1947). *Summa theologica* (p. 1954). Benziger Brothers. http://www.ccel.org/ccel/aquinas/summa

While Islamic theology established human beings as khalifah (vicegerents) on Earth, this concept traditionally carried dual implications of both authority and responsibility. The Islamic principle of mizan (balance) and the concept of amanah (trust) suggest a more complex pattern of interactions between humans and nature than mere dominion. This nuanced theological position has notable implications for contemporary Islamic environmental ethics. This complexity is evident in Islamic scripture, which positions humans as divinely appointed stewards, as evidenced by the Quranic declaration that "Allah made humans 'successors upon the earth' (Qu'ran 6:165) and created the stars for human navigation (e.g. 2:29, 6:96)".[27]

The divergence between Western monotheistic traditions and Eastern religious philosophies regarding human–nature connections reflects fundamentally different cosmological and ontological assumptions. While Western traditions often emphasised hierarchical separation between humans and nature, Eastern traditions typically promoted concepts of interconnectedness and mutual dependence. Several theological traditions offer alternative paradigms that challenge the dominant narrative of human supremacy. The mystical tradition of Sufism within Islam, along with Eastern religious traditions including Daoism, Buddhism, and Hinduism, present more nuanced viewpoints on the human–nature bond. The Buddhist tradition, in particular, offers a striking contrast through its emphasis on universal compassion: "The Eightfold Path of Buddhism uses this concept as a basis for outlining appropriate human conduct toward all creatures and things. It centres on the doctrine of harmlessness or ahimsa which the Jains carried to extremes in their desire to avoid the destruction of any life".[28]

Modern religious thought has witnessed a substantial re-examination of conventional anthropocentric interpretations. Religious scholars and leaders, including figures like Pope Francis with his encyclical "Laudato Si", have begun analysing religious texts through an environmental lens. This theological reorientation suggests the potential for religious traditions to contribute to environmental protection rather than exploitation.

---

27 Moore, B. L. (2017). *Ecological literature and the critique of anthropocentrism* (p. 9). Palgrave Macmillan.

28 Nash, R. (1989). *The rights of nature: A history of environmental ethics* (p. 113). University of Wisconsin Press.

These diverse religious viewpoints on human–nature interactions continue to influence contemporary environmental discourse. The tension between anthropocentric religious interpretations and more balanced spiritual traditions informs current debates about environmental ethics, conservation policies, and the moral status of nature. This religious heritage shapes not only philosophical discussions but also practical approaches to environmental protection and resource management, setting the stage for modern philosophical developments in environmental ethics.

2.1.1.3 Philosophical Evolution of Anthropocentrism: From Classical to Contemporary Thought

The evolution of philosophical anthropocentrism presents a compelling trajectory from ancient Greek thought through modern philosophical discourse. The anthropocentric worldview's theoretical foundations extend to Greek theological conceptions where deities manifested in human form, establishing humanity's central place in cosmic ordering.[29] This early philosophical articulation of human pre-eminence developed well before the emergence of Christian doctrine or Jewish traditions.[30]

Pre-Socratic philosophers formed the essential groundwork for anthropocentric thought through their initial attempts to understand human consciousness and rationality. This early Greek conceptualisation marked the first systematic effort to distinguish human capacities from other natural phenomena, creating a hierarchical understanding that would shape following philosophical traditions.

Classical philosophical discourse developed the core arguments for human exceptionalism that would affect subsequent centuries of Western thought. From Plato and Aristotle to the Stoics, a consistent intellectual thread arose: human possession of rationality, language, the capability of genuine self-determination and moral responsibility justified exclusive moral consideration of human interests.[31] This conceptual structure placed humanity not

---

29 Steiner, G. (2010). *Anthropocentrism and its discontents: The moral status of animals in the history of western philosophy* (p. 1). University of Pittsburgh Press.

30 Moore, B. L. (2017). *Ecological literature and the critique of anthropocentrism* (p. 10). Palgrave Macmillan.

31 Steiner, G. (2010). *Anthropocentrism and its discontents: The moral status of animals in the history of western philosophy* (p. 2). University of Pittsburgh Press.

only as supreme within the natural order but as the sole legitimate bearer of moral status.

While mainstream classical philosophy predominantly supported anthropocentric positions, alternative viewpoints appeared. These early contestations of human dominance, though marginalised, offered vital philosophical counterpoints. For instance, certain Pythagorean schools advocated for the consideration of non-human entities in moral calculations, suggesting early forms of biocentrism.[32]

The Enlightenment period marked a pivotal transformation in anthropocentric philosophy. René Descartes (1596–1650) crystallised this progression by advocating for an absolute separation between human and natural worlds.[33] His mechanistic worldview reduced nature to an automaton, asserting that the "Material world operate like any machine according to fixed and unvarying rules, with laws that have been built into the machine from the start. It has no sentience (if an animal), creativity, or spontaneity of its own".[34] This Cartesian paradigm effectively mechanised animal existence and devalued nature's inherent worth.

The Cartesian separation of mind and matter fundamentally altered Western understanding of human–nature relationships. This dualistic framework not only reinforced anthropocentric assumptions but generated philosophical justifications for environmental exploitation that would later determine industrial development and resource management practices.

John Locke (1632–1704) further advanced this philosophical position, interweaving religious authority with rational justification:

> There cannot be subordination among us … as if we were made for one another's uses, as the inferior ranks of creatures were made for ours … God who hath given the world to men in common hath also given them reason to make use of it to best advantage of life and convenience.[35]

---

32 Sorabji, R. (1993). *Animal minds and human morals: The origins of the western debate* (p. 2). Cornell University Press.

33 Eaton, R. M. (1927). Letter to Henry More. In *Descartes selections*. Scribner.

34 Gillespie, A. (2014). *International environmental law, policy, and ethics* (p. 7). Oxford University Press.

35 Locke, J. (1936). *Two treatises of civil government* (Sections 37, 42–43, 118, 119, 126, 129, 131, 304, 305, 314, 316, 308). Dent; Locke, J. (1998). *An essay concerning human understanding* (Book II, pp. 88–91). Penguin.

The culmination of Enlightenment anthropocentrism found its most sophisticated expression in Immanuel Kant's work. Writing in 1790, Kant declared: "As the single being upon earth that possesses understanding, and, consequently, a capacity for setting before himself ends of his deliberate choice, he is certainly titular lord of nature, and, supposing we regard nature as a teleological system, he is born to be its ultimate end".[36] Kant's critical philosophy vitally shaped the following intellectual period, although some philosophers like Leibniz and Spinoza offered alternative perspectives.

The Scientific Revolution created a paradoxical effect on anthropocentric thought. While Copernican heliocentrism displaced humans from the physical centre of the universe, emerging scientific methodologies reinforced human exceptionalism through their emphasis on rational observation and control over natural phenomena. Modern philosophical discourse has largely preserved these anthropocentric tenets. Bertrand Russell (1872–1970) exemplified this continuity, stating: "And yet I am unable to believe that, in the world as known, there is anything that I can value outside human beings, and, to a much lesser extent, animals".[37] This persistence of anthropocentric thought proves particularly noteworthy given scientific advances that altered humanity's cosmic status. However, scientific evidence of superior human intelligence has served to legitimise enduring human primacy, helping to "explain the presence of anthropocentrism in epistemology and ethics".[38]

Contemporary philosophical discourse sustains strong anthropocentric underpinnings.[39] Modern philosophers like Tibor Machan advocate for human primacy, arguing that "Humans are more important, even better, than other animals, and we deserve the benefits that exploiting animals can provide.... it is right to exploit nature to promote our own lives and happiness".[40]

---

36 Kant, I. (2007). *Critique of judgement* (J. C. Meredith, Trans.; N. Walker, Ed.) (p. 259). Oxford University Press.

37 Russell, B. (2009). My mental development. In R. Egner & L. Denonn (Eds.), *The basic writings of Bertrand Russell* (p. 21). Routledge.

38 Butchvarov, P. (2015). *Anthropocentrism in philosophy: Realism, antirealism, semirealism* (p. 6). De Gruyter.

39 Boyd, D. R. (2017). *The rights of nature: A legal revolution that could save the world* (p. xxv). ECW Press.

40 Machan, T. R. (2004). *Putting humans first: Why we are nature's favorite* (p. 116). Rowman & Littlefield.

The lasting impact of traditional anthropocentric philosophy on contemporary environmental discourse reveals an essential tension. While these established philosophical frameworks persist in shaping legal and policy approaches to environmental protection, emerging ecological challenges increasingly illuminate their limitations. This dynamic between historical philosophical legitimisation of human dominance and growing recognition of ecological interdependence sets the stage for modern environmental ethics.

2.1.1.4 Contemporary Manifestations and Legal Framework

The theoretical foundations of anthropocentrism find their most tangible expression in modern legal and institutional structures. While the inferior-superior relationship between humans and the universe appears across philosophical, political, social, and economic domains, its most consequential impact emerges in environmental law and policy. Notably, this legal expression presents a complex paradox: although anthropocentric in origin and justification, it does not preclude environmental protection. Instead, it reconceptualises such protection through the lens of human interests.

The emergence of modern environmental law in the mid-twentieth century marked a significant shift in legal mechanisms for nature. While maintaining anthropocentric foundations, this period witnessed the first systematic attempts to create comprehensive environmental governance systems. This development reflected growing awareness of environmental degradation's potential impact on human welfare rather than any basic shift away from anthropocentric values.

The institutionalisation of environmental protection measures, both nationally and internationally, operates fundamentally within an anthropocentric paradigm. This structure becomes evident through an examination of pivotal international environmental conventions and legal documents. Key expressions of this anthropocentric orientation include declarations "to protect and improve the environment for present and future generations",[41] and the explicit assertion that "of all things in the world, people are the most precious".[42]

---

41 United Nations. (1972). *Report of the United Nations conference on the human environment* (A/CONF.48/14/Rev.1, Principle 1).

42 United Nations. (1972). *Report of the United Nations conference on the human environment* (A/CONF.48/14/Rev.1, p. 70).

The emphasis on human benefit in environmental law reveals an essential friction between instrumental and intrinsic value viewpoints to nature. While some legal scholars advocate for recognising nature's inherent worth, existing legal systems predominantly operate through the lens of human utility, measuring environmental protection's value through its benefits to human society.

The European legal system particularly exemplifies this anthropocentric perspective, stating that "as befits the genius of Europe, particular attention will be given to ... protecting the environment so that progress may really be put at the service of mankind".[43] This regional articulation mirrors broader international principles, as evidenced in global declarations that "human beings are at the centre of concerns for sustainable development".[44] Such anthropocentric foundations extend to development policies, which explicitly "make the human being the main participant and beneficiary of development".[45]

The practical application of anthropocentric environmental law confronts several distinct issues. First, defining environmental damage purely through human impacts may overlook crucial ecological degradation that doesn't immediately affect human interests. Second, the emphasis on human benefit can lead to short-term decision-making that undermines long-term ecosystem stability.

The pervasive influence of anthropocentric thought, cultivated over millennia, now emerges as the primary conceptual model in environmental law. This practical execution reveals a crucial distinction: environmental protection measures, while ostensibly focused on preserving natural systems, ultimately serve human interests. Conservation efforts, pollution prevention

---

[43] Council of the European Communities. (1973). *Declaration of the council of the european communities on the program of action of the european community on the environment* (73/C 112/01, Part 1, Introduction, para. 3).

[44] United Nations. (1992). *Rio declaration on environment and development* (A/CONF.151/26, Principle 1).

[45] United Nations. (1986). *Declaration on the right to development* (A/RES/41/128, para. 13).

initiatives, and resource management strategies derive their legal and policy justifications from their instrumental value to humanity.[46]

The dominance of Western anthropocentric legal structures in international environmental law presents specific difficulties for Global South nations, where different cultural and philosophical traditions often embrace more integrated views of human–nature relationships. This discord becomes evident in international environmental negotiations and policy execution.

Recent developments in environmental law suggest potential evolution beyond purely anthropocentric systems. The emergence of rights of nature legislation in various jurisdictions, along with growing recognition of indigenous perspectives on environmental protection, indicates possible pathways toward more balanced legal approaches. However, these alternatives must still operate within predominantly anthropocentric legal arrangements.

The evolution of international environmental law thus reveals both the practical utility and inherent limitations of anthropocentric approaches to environmental protection. While this structure has enabled significant environmental protection measures, its basic orientation toward human interests may prove insufficient for addressing emerging ecological challenges that require recognition of nature's intrinsic value beyond its utility to human society. This conflict between established anthropocentric legal structures and emerging ecological imperatives sets the stage for potential transformative changes in environmental law. The challenge lies in developing legal systems that can effectively bridge anthropocentric institutional foundations with growing recognition of ecological interconnectedness.

2.1.2 Capitalism and Environmental Degradation: A Critical Analysis

2.1.2.1 Fundamental Tensions: Capitalism's View of Nature

The conceptualisation of nature within capitalist systems reveals fundamental tensions between economic imperatives and ecological realities. At its core, capitalism, as defined by Giddens, represents "a system of commodity production, centred upon the relation between private ownership of capital

[46] Gillespie, A. (2014). *International environmental law, policy, and ethics* (p. 13). Oxford University Press.

and propertyless wage labour".[47] This economic structure extends beyond human labour relations to encompass the natural world, converting ecological elements into marketable commodities.

This essential understanding of capitalism illuminates how the system inherently converts not only human labour but also natural processes into marketable commodities. In this context, plants, animals, water, and minerals acquire value primarily as "natural capital", representing both the stock value of natural assets and the potential flow of goods and services these assets can generate.[48] The concept of "natural capital" emerged as an attempt to quantify and incorporate environmental elements into economic calculations, yet this very process reinforces the anthropocentric view of nature as merely an economic resource.

The historical shift from viewing nature as life-sustaining to commodity represents a significant departure from pre-industrial economic systems. This change occurred parallel to the Industrial Revolution, marking a decisive shift from viewing nature as a source of sustenance to seeing it as a repository of raw materials for industrial production. Industrialisation and its associated consumption patterns, fundamentally shaped by capitalist modes of production, demonstrate direct causality with contemporary ecological crises.[49] This relationship exemplifies the intrinsically anthropocentric character of capitalist systems. Nature, reconceptualised as human property, becomes merely a resource base for exploitation and immediate profit generation.[50] In this paradigm, ecological preservation and natural systems' regenerative capacity become subordinate considerations to profit maximisation.

The institution of private property rights, a cornerstone of capitalist systems, further complicates the relationship between economic development and environmental protection. These rights bestow upon property owners

---

[47] Giddens, A. (1990). *The consequences of modernity* (p. 55). Polity Press.

[48] Hanna, S., Folke, C., & Maler, K. G. (Eds.). (1996). *Rights to nature: Ecological, economic, cultural, and political principles of institutions for the environment* (p. 40). Island Press.

[49] Murray, J. (2014). Earth jurisprudence, wild law, emergent law: The emerging field of ecology and law – Part 1. *Liverpool Law Review, 35*, 215–231 (p. 220). https://doi.org/10.1007/s10991-014-9148-1

[50] Murray, J. (2014). Earth jurisprudence, wild law, emergent law: The emerging field of ecology and law – Part 1. *Liverpool Law Review, 35*, 215–231 (p. 220). https://doi.org/10.1007/s10991-014-9148-1

nearly unlimited authority over resource utilisation, including the prerogative to exploit or destroy natural resources, potentially against broader community interests. This legal structure renders natural resources fundamentally vulnerable, lacking inherent protections against destructive exploitation.[51] The privatisation of nature through property rights systems creates particular challenges for environmental protection. Unlike human-made commodities, natural resources and ecological systems operate as interconnected networks that transcend property boundaries. This inherent mismatch between legal structures and ecological realities undermines proper environmental stewardship.

The globalisation of capitalist systems has universalised this commodified approach to nature, affecting environmental governance worldwide. Developing nations, especially, face intensified pressure to sacrifice environmental protection for economic development, creating a false dichotomy between ecological preservation and economic progress. The capitalist approach to nature reveals significant problems in market valuation mechanisms. Many ecological services and natural processes resist monetary quantification, leading to their systematic undervaluation or complete exclusion from economic calculations. This limitation becomes especially problematic when attempting to assess long-term environmental impacts.

The conversion of nature into commodity reveals three critical tensions inherent in capitalist approaches to environmental management:

1. The conflict between short-term profit maximisation and long-term ecological sustainability
2. The disconnect between private property rights and the inherently interconnected nature of ecological systems
3. The fundamental contradiction between treating nature as boundless resource and its finite reality

While some scholars advocate for reform within capitalist systems through improved valuation methods and stronger regulations, others argue that the essential tension between capitalism's growth imperative and ecological sustainability requires more radical systemic changes. This debate raises crucial

[51] Wissenburg, M. (2006). Liberalism. In A. Dobson & R. Eckersley (Eds.), *Political theory and the ecological challenge* (p. 22). Cambridge University Press.

questions about the possibility of reconciling capitalist economic structures with effective environmental protection.

2.1.2.2 The Growth Paradox: Unlimited Expansion vs. Natural Limits

The central paradox of capitalist economic structures emerges from an inherent contradiction between the imperative for unlimited economic growth and the finite nature of Earth's resources. This structural incompatibility manifests most acutely in the free market system which, despite being proposed as an intermediary mechanism for resource allocation, ultimately proves inherently incompatible with the limited natural resources upon which it depends.[52]

The ideology of unlimited economic growth, crystallised during the Industrial Revolution and institutionalised throughout the twentieth century, transformed the connection between economic operations and natural resources. This transformation established a paradigm where economic progress became inextricably linked to escalating resource exploitation, creating systemic environmental pressures that transcend normal market corrections.

The institutional architecture supporting this contradiction involves complex state-market dynamics. Nation-states, while nominally responsible for environmental protection and conservation within their territories, remain historically intertwined with capitalist expansion. This dynamic manifests through policies promoting increased material consumption, precisely the practices that draw environmental criticism.[53] The resulting governance structure creates a problematic configuration where environmental protection inevitably yields to growth imperatives, compromising long-term environmental stability for short-term economic gains.

The theoretical defence of capitalist growth models rests primarily on the premise that continuous accumulation of new products and services, coupled with improved productivity, will benefit consumers through lower prices and

---

[52] Murray, J. (2014). Earth jurisprudence, wild law, emergent law: The emerging field of ecology and law – Part 1. *Liverpool Law Review, 35*, 215–231 (p. 220, para. 5). https://doi.org/10.1007/s10991-014-9148-1

[53] Hurrell, A. (2006). The state. In A. Dobson & R. Eckersley (Eds.), *Political theory and the ecological challenge* (p. 170). Cambridge University Press.

increased accessibility.[54] However, this assumption inherently misconstrues the connection between economic activity and natural systems. While the social and economic benefits of this system remain debatable, its detrimental impact on natural systems has emerged as an empirically verifiable reality.

This environmental degradation stems largely from critical misconceptions in traditional economic theory. Classical economists operated under the flawed assumption of infinite resources, positing that market functions would naturally regulate resource use through price signals – as resources become scarce, rising prices would automatically reduce demand.[55] This theoretical framework contains a critical oversight: market operations consistently fail to account for environmental thresholds and irreversible environmental damage. More fundamentally, no price mechanism can resolve the ultimate limitation: once a resource is exhausted, no market adjustment can restore it.

The failure of market operations extends beyond simple resource depletion to encompass broader systemic inadequacies. Markets consistently undervalue environmental services, fail to internalise environmental externalities, and ignore critical threshold effects in natural systems. This persistent undervaluation creates a dangerous disconnect between economic indicators of growth and the actual state of environmental resources.

2.1.2.3 The True Cost of Capitalist Production

Traditional economic theory's critical flaw extends beyond resource limitations to a more pernicious assumption: that Earth's capacity to absorb industrial impacts is limitless.[56] This misconception enabled unprecedented industrial expansion without environmental oversight, resulting in irreversible ecological damage before the recognition of natural systems' finite absorption capacity.

The concept of environmental externalities emerged gradually as economists began recognising the constraints of traditional market pricing.

---

54 McNally, R., & Wheale, P. (1994). Environmental and medical bioethics in late modernity: Anthony Giddens, genetic engineering and the post-modern state. In R. Attfield & A. Belsey (Eds.), *Philosophy and the natural environment* (p. 215). Cambridge University Press.

55 Baker, N. (2007). Rebalancing the system: An agenda for change. *Environmental Law & Management, 19*, 77–81.

56 Baker, N. (2007). Rebalancing the system: An agenda for change. *Environmental Law & Management, 19*, 77–81.

This theoretical development marked a crucial shift in understanding capitalism's true operational costs, though this recognition has not translated into systematic reform of pricing mechanisms.

The disparity between market prices and actual costs exemplifies capitalism's systematic undervaluation of environmental impacts. Consider the apparently simple case of a tomato: its true cost encompasses not merely the point-of-purchase price but also the cumulative environmental externalities generated throughout its production cycle. These hidden costs include atmospheric pollution from production and transportation processes, depletion of water resources, and soil degradation from pesticide use. The complexity requires a thorough analysis considering multiple layers of environmental degradation: resource depletion at the point of production, cumulative impacts throughout the supply chain, long-term effects on ecosystem services, and the often irreversible nature of environmental damage. This multi-dimensional cost structure reveals how conventional market pricing systematically obscures environmental impacts.

Market-based environmental solutions represent attempts to internalise externalities within existing capitalist frameworks. These approaches, while acknowledging environmental costs, ultimately reinforce the commodification of nature by translating ecological values into market terms. Contemporary attempts to address these systemic failures through market mechanisms reflect capitalism's inherent constraints. Neo-capitalist solutions, including "carbon offset credits, debt-for-nature swaps, ethical consumerism, green design, and financializing nature", paradoxically attempt to resolve environmental degradation through the very market mechanisms that precipitated the ecological crisis.[57]

The temporal dimension of environmental costs presents another critical challenge. Market mechanisms predominantly focus on immediate or short-term costs, failing to adequately account for long-term environmental degradation or intergenerational impacts. This temporal myopia compounds the systematic undervaluation of environmental resources and reinforces the inherent inadequacy of market-based solutions.

---

[57] Demos, T. J. (2015). Rights of nature: Art and ecology in the Americas. In *Rights of nature* [Exhibition catalog]. Nottingham Contemporary.

Alternative approaches to cost assessment, incorporating ecological economics principles, suggest holistic frameworks for evaluating environmental impacts. These models challenge traditional cost–benefit analyses by emphasising ecological interconnectedness and the irreplaceable nature of certain environmental services. However, these approaches prove inadequate precisely because they emerge from and perpetuate a system predicated on nature's subordination and exploitation. The recognition of capitalism's true environmental costs necessitates comprehensive reconsideration of current economic policies and regulatory frameworks. While market-based solutions may offer temporary mitigation, addressing the full scope of environmental costs requires more profound systemic changes.

The systematic undervaluation of environmental costs within capitalist frameworks necessitates examination of how different philosophical approaches attempt to reconcile economic and ecological imperatives. Among these, utilitarian philosophy emerges as particularly significant, both for its historical influence on economic thought and its continued impact on environmental policymaking. While utilitarianism initially served to justify resource exploitation through cost–benefit calculations, its evolution has generated more nuanced approaches to environmental valuation. This philosophical framework provides crucial insights into how societies attempt to balance human welfare with environmental protection, though it ultimately reveals similar limitations to purely market-based approaches. Understanding these limitations and possibilities requires systematic examination of utilitarian approaches to nature, particularly as they inform contemporary environmental policy and law.

2.1.3 Utilitarian Approaches to Nature

2.1.3.1 Classical Utilitarianism: From Human Happiness to Animal Suffering

The systematic development of utilitarian thought, rooted in hedonist philosophy and Human traditions, achieved its formal expression in the eighteenth and nineteenth centuries through the works of Jeremy Bentham and John Stuart Mill.[58] Though contemporary interpretations have diversified,

[58] Driver, J. (2014). The history of utilitarianism. In E. N. Zalta (Ed.), *The Stanford encyclopedia of philosophy* (Winter 2014 ed.). https://plato.stanford.edu/archives/win2014/entries/utilitarianism-history/.

classical utilitarianism's essential principle centred on achieving "the greatest happiness for the greatest number".[59] Significantly, this formulation initially confined its consideration to "currently living humans", establishing a framework that would later draw ecological critique.

The principle of utility provided a "standard of right and wrong" according to which all our choices should promote the greatest happiness of all those whose interest is in question.[60] Its practical application to natural spaces reveals its inherent anthropocentric orientation. The protection of green spaces illustrates this dynamic: under utilitarian calculus, preservation depends entirely on balancing human enjoyment against resource utility. Such calculations legitimise environmental protection only when it generates ongoing human benefit. Consequently, moral permission – even obligation – exists to exploit resources for human advantage, regardless of ecological consequences.[61] This approach, elevating current human interests above future generations, animals, and natural systems, continues to shape contemporary economic policy, environmental law, and international agreements.

Despite its anthropocentric foundations and inherent hierarchy between living human beings and other entities, classical utilitarian thought under Bentham and Mill's leadership introduced groundbreaking theoretical recognition of animal welfare through its emphasis on pleasure and pain.[62] Bentham's vital inquiry – "the question, is not, Can they reason? nor Can they talk? but Can they suffer?"[63] – challenged existing legal frameworks excluding animal protection. Through prioritising the capacity for suffering over rational capabilities or linguistic expression,[64] Bentham developed a more

---

59 Emmeneger, S., & Tschentscher, A. (1994). Taking nature's rights seriously: The long way to biocentrism in environmental law. *Georgetown International Environmental Law Review, 6*(3), 545–742.

60 Steiner, G. (2010). *Anthropocentrism and its discontents: The moral status of animals in the history of western philosophy* (p. 162). University of Pittsburgh Press.

61 Emmeneger, S., & Tschentscher, A. (1994). Taking nature's rights seriously: The long way to biocentrism in environmental law. *Georgetown International Environmental Law Review, 6*(3), 545–742.

62 Steiner, G. (2010). *Anthropocentrism and its discontents: The moral status of animals in the history of western philosophy* (pp. 154–155). University of Pittsburgh Press.

63 Bentham, J. (1948). *An introduction to the principles of morals and legislation* (p. 311). Nabu Press.

64 Steiner, G. (2010). *Anthropocentrism and its discontents: The moral status of animals in the history of western philosophy* (p. 163). University of Pittsburgh Press.

inclusive ethical framework, rendering utilitarianism less anthropocentric than contemporary deontological approaches. Bentham and Mill's conclusions acknowledged that "animals figure in our moral calculus, that in many instances the happiness and suffering of animals create obligations on our part to treat animals in certain ways, and that these obligations are directly to the animals in question rather than to humanity".[65]

Mill expanded this theoretical framework through a significant question about human moral responsibility toward animals: "Granted that any practice causes more pain to animals than it gives pleasure to man; is that practice moral or immoral? And if, exactly in proportion as human beings raise their heads out of the slough of selfishness, they do not with one voice answer 'immoral,' let the morality of the principle of utility be forever condemned".[66] This theoretical position aligns with the broader evolution of rights theory during the humanist movement, marking a transformation from dismissal of non-human interests toward nuanced moral calculation. Yet it fell short of advocating equality, raising essential questions about establishing rational balance between human pleasures and animal suffering.

Mill's challenge to the traditional religious notion of nature's purpose represents another significant theoretical development, one that would shape the philosophical understanding of human–nature relationships. He argued: "The scheme of Nature regarded in its whole extent, cannot have had, for its sole or even principal object, the good of human or other sentient beings. What good it brings to them, is mostly the result of their own exertions. Whatsoever, in nature, gives indication of beneficent design, proves this beneficence to be armed only with limited power; and the duty of man is to co-operate with the beneficent powers, not by imitating but by perpetually striving to amend the course of nature – and bringing that part of it over which we can exercise control, more nearly into conformity with a high standard of justice and goodness".[67] Although this argument challenged

---

65 Steiner, G. (2010). *Anthropocentrism and its discontents: The moral status of animals in the history of western philosophy* (p. 155). University of Pittsburgh Press.

66 Mill, J. S. (1985). Utilitarianism. In J. M. Robson (Ed.), *The collected works of John Stuart Mill, Volume X: Essays on ethics, religion, and society* (p. 245). University of Toronto Press. (Original work published 1861).

67 Mill, J. S. (n.d.). Nature. In L. J. Matz (Ed.), *Three essays on religion* (pp. 103–104). Broadview Editions.

Stoic-Christian dogma, it paradoxically reinforced human dominion. Mill "categorically rejects all idealized views of nature and instead reduces nature to instrumentality",[68] deriving this position partly from his assessment of humans' superior capacity for suffering. For this reason, the lives of animals are considered less valuable than the lives of people.[69]

2.1.3.2 Contemporary Utilitarianism's Evolution: Expanding Moral Consideration

The evolution of utilitarian thought regarding nature finds its most sophisticated contemporary expression in Peter Singer's theoretical reformulation of utility. Singer's distinctive contribution lies in his reconceptualisation of utility beyond the classical parameters of pleasure and pain, expanding it to encompass "the interest of those affected".[70] This advancement transforms the foundational question from one of sensory experience to one of interest-bearing ability, marking a notable shift in utilitarian thought.

This reconceptualisation extends beyond mere expansion of classical utilitarian principles; it fundamentally alters the basis for moral status. Where classical utilitarianism emphasised pleasure and pain as measurable quantities, Singer's approach introduces a nuanced understanding of interests as qualitative states of being. His structure establishes rigorous criteria: entities must possess subjectivity or selfhood to qualify for moral consideration. Within this theoretical construct, all sentient beings – defined by their ability to suffer or experience pleasure – meet the threshold for ethical inclusion.[71]

The establishment of interests rather than mere sensation as the basis for moral standing allows for a sophisticated understanding of animal welfare, yet paradoxically constrains the scope of environmental protection through its emphasis on sentience. This reformulation marks a vital departure from classical positions that subordinated animal interests to human benefit.

---

68 Steiner, G. (2010). *Anthropocentrism and its discontents: The moral status of animals in the history of western philosophy* (pp. 164–165). University of Pittsburgh Press.

69 Steiner, G. (2010). *Anthropocentrism and its discontents: The moral status of animals in the history of western philosophy* (p. 166). University of Pittsburgh Press.

70 Singer, P. (1993). *Practical ethics* (2nd ed.) (pp. 12,14). Cambridge University Press.

71 Steiner, G. (2010). *Anthropocentrism and its discontents: The moral status of animals in the history of western philosophy* (p. 6). University of Pittsburgh Press.

Under Singer's approach, animals possess intrinsic moral worth through their ability to have interests, independent of human utility calculations.

Singer's theoretical innovation manifests in contemporary debates about environmental protection and animal welfare. While establishing stronger philosophical grounds for animal rights, this approach reveals inherent constraints when addressing broader ecological concerns, particularly ecosystem protection and biodiversity conservation. Despite expanding ethical consideration beyond traditional human-centred boundaries, his emphasis on sentience as the criterion for moral status explicitly excludes mountains, ecosystems, and other non-sentient natural entities from direct ethical consideration.

This boundary becomes especially pronounced when confronting modern environmental challenges, where protecting entire ecosystems and non-sentient natural entities proves crucial for environmental sustainability. Their preservation derives legitimacy solely through instrumental value to sentient beings, primarily humans, thus maintaining a refined form of anthropocentric valuation. These persistent challenges in accommodating non-sentient nature within utilitarian structures, even in their most evolved forms, indicate fundamental constraints in utility-based approaches to environmental protection.

2.1.3.3 Critical Analysis of Utilitarian Approaches

The utilitarian framework for environmental and animal protection reveals inherent constraints in both theoretical construction and practical application. A critical weakness emerges in the methodology of interest assessment, particularly in scenarios involving multifaceted moral trade-offs. These evaluative issues have persisted throughout utilitarian theory's development, intensifying as environmental concerns grow more intricate. Traditional utilitarian approaches, designed for relatively straightforward human welfare assessments, prove insufficient when addressing ecological issues involving diverse species, ecosystem services, and intergenerational impacts.

This insufficiency becomes evident in paradigmatic cases: Suppose, for example, an experiment that sacrificed a thousand monkeys, after considerable suffering, leads to the development of an antidote that could cure three children of a very rare and uncomfortable but not dangerous disease. In this case, how would one calculate the greatest good for the greatest number?[72]

---

[72] Hoch, D. (1987). Environmental ethics and nonhuman interests: A challenge to anthropocentric license. *Gonzaga Law Review, 23*, 331–347.

These multi-layered ethical considerations encompass temporal dimensions (immediate animal suffering versus potential future benefits), numerical comparisons (quantity of lives versus intensity of benefit), and qualitative distinctions (animal suffering versus human comfort). Such evaluations resist meaningful quantification within any systematic framework. The task of measuring and comparing fundamentally different types of interests remains unresolved. Moreover, the utilitarian emphasis on "greatest number" privileges quantitative considerations over qualitative ethical claims, systematically diminishing the significance of individual rights and interests.[73]

These methodological issues expose essential flaws in utilitarian approaches to environmental ethics. The inability to adequately measure diverse interests undermines the theoretical basis of utilitarian environmental decision-making. Such theoretical constraints materialise concretely in contemporary environmental law and policy. While utilitarian principles have shaped environmental protection frameworks, they generate persistent structural problems. Environmental legislation, based on utilitarian assessments, attempts to balance human needs for clean air, water, and adequate green spaces against demands for economic development, industrial growth, and urbanisation.

Present-day environmental issues, including climate change, biodiversity loss, and ecosystem degradation, reveal complex interdependencies between immediate human interests, long-term ecological stability, and the inherent value of natural systems. These relationships transcend simple utility metrics, exposing fundamental limitations in utilitarian evaluations. The current environmental legal framework, operating within this utilitarian paradigm, mediates between preservation and development imperatives, yet inherently reduces environmental protection to anthropocentric utility assessments.

The resultant framework creates a system where environmental protection depends entirely on demonstrable human benefit, evaluated through simplified cost–benefit analyses. This reduction of ecological complexity to economic computation leaves crucial environmental decisions vulnerable to market-driven imperatives. This analysis demonstrates the imperative for supplementary or alternative frameworks capable of addressing the intricate nature of environmental protection, particularly regarding non-quantifiable ecological values and intergenerational environmental interests.

---

73 Hoch, D. (1987). Environmental ethics and nonhuman interests: A challenge to anthropocentric license. *Gonzaga Law Review, 23*, 331–347 (pp. 335–336).

Such theoretical evolution appears essential for addressing contemporary environmental challenges that exceed the analytical capacity of traditional utilitarian approaches.

2.1.4 The Evolution of Environmental Ethics

2.1.4.1 The Development of Modern Environmentalism

Environmental ethics emerged as a distinct theoretical discipline in the late 1800s, as pioneering philosophers and scientists articulated initial critiques of prevailing human–nature relationships. Despite providing systematic analysis of anthropogenic environmental modification, these early intellectual contributions remained peripheral to contemporary intellectual discourse, their significance unrealised for nearly a century.[74]

This conceptual dormancy persisted until the post-War industrial expansion precipitated a transformative shift, culminating in the 1960s and 1970s with unprecedented evidence of ecological degradation. This era witnessed the convergence of multiple catalysts: emerging social movements (anti-war, anti-nuclear), escalating environmental deterioration, and growing recognition of these impacts on human welfare. The manifestation of ecological consequences in tangible human terms catalysed widespread societal reassessment. This period marked a decisive transformation in public consciousness, as collective discourse began systematically examining resource exploitation patterns, their immediate and long-term consequences, and the essential nature of human-environmental interactions, particularly within the broader critique of capitalism.

Public consciousness of environmental imperatives intensified significantly during this period, manifesting through increasingly assertive demands for environmental protection and enhanced living conditions. Newly established non-governmental organisations emerged as instrumental actors, initiating systematic governmental lobbying and corporate accountability campaigns.

---

[74] In 1854: Henry David Thoreau wrote Walden. In 1864: George Perkins Marsh's Man and Nature is published, a foundational study of scientific conservation. In 1866: Ernst Haeckel coins the term ecology. In 1892: John Muir cofounds the Sierra Club. For a more detailed timeline, please see Peterson Del Mar, D. (2006). *Environmentalism* (p. xii). Pearson Longman; Dauvergne, P. (2009). *The A to Z of environmentalism* (pp. xxiv-xxv). Scarecrow Press.

These coordinated initiatives transformed ecological concerns from peripheral considerations to central positions in national and international political agendas, particularly as global-scale environmental issues gained unprecedented prominence in policy discourse.[75]

This heightened environmental awareness catalysed the development of innovative conceptual constructs addressing the unrestrained exploitation of natural resources, which had proceeded without effective legal restrictions or regulatory oversight. A pivotal transformation emerged in environmental protection methodologies: from market-oriented solutions, predicated on liberal economic theory's assertion that market forces could resolve all social challenges, including ecological degradation, to state-centred approaches emphasising governmental responsibility for environmental and natural resource protection. This intellectual evolution established modern environmentalism as a comprehensive paradigm, integrating multiple systems of thought into a coherent framework for understanding human–environment relationships.[76]

Modern environmentalism, as a meta-theoretical construct, transcends conventional environmental protection to address essential questions about human existence and our relationship with the natural world. Its conceptual architecture derives from critical ontological considerations that examine not merely how humans interact with nature, but humanity's very position within the cosmic order. This ontological foundation establishes the basis for the widely acknowledged, though not exhaustive, distinction between radical and non-radical orientations in environmental thought. From this theoretical matrix emerge two distinct trajectories: non-radical environmentalism, designated as the "light green movement", encompasses techno-centric (reformist) methodologies privileging technological solutions within existing societal structures, and bio-centric viewpoints extending limited moral consideration to non-human entities. In contrast, radical environmentalism, termed the "dark green movement" and manifesting through eco-centrism, presents an alternative paradigm that inherently challenges existing human–nature relationships.

---

75 Dauvergne, P. (2009). *The A to Z of environmentalism* (p. xliv). Scarecrow Press.

76 Elliott, L. (2018). Environmentalism. In *Encyclopædia Britannica*. https://www.britannica.com/topic/environmentalism

The non-radical orientation, which "argues for a managerial approach to environmental problems, secure in the belief that they can be solved without essential changes in present values or patterns of production and consumption"[77] has achieved intellectual and institutional predominance in contemporary political and legal structures. This perspective posits that ecological issues can be effectively addressed through existing societal systems and calibrated reforms within current institutional frameworks. Its proponents maintain that technological advancement and market dynamics, subject to appropriate regulatory oversight, can resolve environmental concerns without requiring systemic reconstruction. This conceptual orientation has established itself as the prevailing paradigm for environmental protection in contemporary governance, shaping both policy development and legislative initiatives.

In distinct theoretical contrast, ecocentric perspectives assert that "a sustainable and fulfilling existence presupposes radical changes in our relationship with the non-human natural world, and in our mode of social and political life".[78] This intellectual stance necessitates comprehensive reconceptualisation of established human–nature relationships and existing societal structures, categorically rejecting the sufficiency of incremental reforms. The essential divergence between these orientations extends beyond methodological preferences to encompass primary differences in their understanding of ecological challenges, their origins, and their potential solutions.

Within the broader ecocentric tradition, distinct theoretical branches have evolved, each offering unique analytical frameworks for understanding and addressing environmental challenges. Deep ecology emphasises the intrinsic value of natural systems, advocating for a core reconstitution of human society's relationship with nature. Social ecology examines environmental issues through the analysis of societal configurations and power relationships, positioning ecological degradation as a consequence of social hierarchies and patterns of domination. Eco-feminism provides a distinctive analytical approach, examining environmental deterioration through the lens of gender-based power relations and patriarchal social structures.[79] These diverse

77 Dobson, A. (2007). *Green political thought* (p. 2). Routledge.
78 Dobson, A. (2007). *Green political thought* (p. 3). Routledge.
79 Elliott, L. (2018). Environmentalism. In *Encyclopædia Britannica*. https://www.britannica.com/topic/environmentalism

theoretical orientations, while united in their substantive critique of current environmental relationships, offer varied perspectives on both the origins of ecological crisis and potential trajectories toward environmental sustainability, collectively enriching the theoretical landscape of environmental ethics.

2.1.4.2 Non-Radical Environmental Thought

Non-radical environmentalism constitutes a widely accepted conceptual paradigm that defines environmentalism as a "political and ethical movement that seeks to improve and protect the quality of the natural environment".[80] While emerging as a response to environmental degradation, this framework maintains significant elements of the anthropocentric worldview discussed previously, particularly in its approach to human–nature relationships. Within this non-radical construct, the primary methodological approaches focus on two distinct yet interrelated objectives: to "forge new relationship between humans and the natural systems which support life on this planet"[81] and to transform environmentally harmful human activities through modified political, economic, and social organisational structures.[82] These theoretical principles have materialised through systematic applied initiatives, as heightened public consciousness and non-governmental organisation efforts have catalysed the implementation of scientific resource management strategies aimed at optimising natural resource utilisation while minimising environmental degradation.[83] This strategic implementation manifests through specific interventions such as "recycling, the use of alternative energy technologies, the decentralisation and democratisation of economic and social planning",[84] representing concrete attempts to address environmental challenges within existing societal frameworks without fundamentally challenging their underlying anthropocentric assumptions.

---

80 Elliott, L. (2018). Environmentalism. In *Encyclopædia Britannica* (para. 1). https://www.britannica.com/topic/environmentalism.

81 Tarlock, A. D. (2009). History of environmental law. In A. D. Tarlock & J. C. Dembach (Eds.), *Environmental laws and their enforcement* (Vol. 1, pp. 41–65). Encyclopedia of Life Support Systems.

82 Elliott, L. (2018). Environmentalism. In *Encyclopædia Britannica*. https://www.britannica.com/topic/environmentalism.

83 Dauvergne, P. (2009). *The A to Z of environmentalism* (p. xliii). Scarecrow Press.

84 Elliott, L. (2018). Environmentalism. In *Encyclopædia Britannica*. https://www.britannica.com/topic/environmentalism.

While "environmentalism claims that living things other than humans, and the natural environment as a whole, are deserving of consideration in reasoning about the morality of political, economic, and social policies",[85] this broader ethical claim primarily characterises radical environmental movements rather than light green environmentalism. The non-radical approach extends moral consideration to the non-human world only insofar as it pertains to conscious entities,[86] reflecting its distinctive philosophical boundaries and revealing its continued adherence to traditional anthropocentric hierarchies. This selective extension of moral consideration illustrates a crucial distinction between radical and non-radical environmental thought: while both acknowledge environmental challenges, their philosophical foundations and proposed solutions diverge fundamentally in their understanding of nature's moral status and humanity's relationship with the natural world.

Bio-centric environmentalism, as a specific manifestation of non-radical thought, particularly "would seem to miss the point of much concern about wild nature; that concern simply does not seem to have as its focus the rights of such items as trees, fungi, gnats, rocks and stalactites, or, more grandly, species, ecosystems and the biosphere".[87] This philosophical orientation illuminates several critical aspects of the non-radical approach: its emphasis on pragmatic solutions rather than comprehensive theoretical reconceptualisation, its maintenance of traditional hierarchies in ecological consideration, and its tendency to address environmental issues within existing paradigms of human–nature relationships. Such an orientation, while potentially effective for addressing immediate environmental concerns, represents an incremental modification of anthropocentric perspectives rather than the fundamental systemic transformation that contemporary ecological challenges might require.

---

[85] Elliott, L. (2018). Environmentalism. In *Encyclopædia Britannica* (para. 1). https://www.britannica.com/topic/environmentalism.

[86] Elliot, R. (1994). Ecology and the ethics of environmental restoration. In R. Attfield & A. Belsey (Eds.), *Philosophy and the natural environment* (Royal Institute of Philosophy Supplement 36, pp. 31–43). Cambridge University Press.

[87] Elliot, R. (1994). Ecology and the ethics of environmental restoration. In R. Attfield & A. Belsey (Eds.), *Philosophy and the natural environment* (Royal Institute of Philosophy Supplement 36, p. 35). Cambridge University Press.

The assessment of non-radical environmentalism as an ideological structure necessitates examination against established criteria for ideological systems:

> They must provide an analytical description of society… Second, they must prescribe a particular form of society employing beliefs about the human condition that sustain and reproduce views about nature of the prescribed society. Finally, they must provide a programme for political action, or show how to get from the society we currently inhabit to the one prescribed by the ideology in question.[88]

When evaluated against these ideological criteria, non-radical environmentalism demonstrates significant structural insufficiencies that extend beyond mere practical limitations to reveal fundamental theoretical constraints. Despite identifying resource scarcity as a central concern, the light green movement characteristically neglects deeper investigation into the socio-economic origins of this scarcity and its complex interconnections with broader questions of social justice and resource distribution. This selective focus illustrates a crucial limitation: while non-radical environmentalism acknowledges environmental problems, it often fails to engage with their underlying systemic causes, instead remaining primarily focused on the immediate phenomena of species extinction and resource depletion, thereby perpetuating rather than challenging existing socio-economic structures.

Within the domain of resource management, the applied expressions of non-radical environmental thought have concentrated predominantly on technical interventions and market-based solutions: "practically the totality of environmentalists efforts has gone into suggesting ways of reducing the consumption of non-renewable resources, increasing the use of renewable resources, and reducing the amount of waste generated by industrial and other processes".[89] This technical orientation, while offering immediate practical utility and measurable outcomes, reveals inherent inadequacies in addressing fundamental ecological challenges. The emphasis on technological solutions and efficiency improvements, though valuable for immediate environmental

---

88 Dobson, A. (2007). *Green political thought* (p. 3). Routledge.

89 Dobson, A. (1998). *Justice and the environment: Conceptions of environmental sustainability and theories of distributive justice* (p. 13). Oxford University Press.

protection, often serves to reinforce existing economic paradigms that prioritise growth over ecological sustainability.

The subsequent emergence of the environmental justice movement marked a significant departure from classic light green environmentalism, specifically addressing these previously neglected societal dimensions and power relationships.[90] This evolution in environmental thought highlighted the limitations of purely technical approaches and emphasised the need for more comprehensive social and political analysis. The examination of environmental law and multilateral environmental agreements developed within this non-ecocentric paradigm reveals substantial deficiencies in generating lasting solutions to contemporary ecological challenges. These legal and policy frameworks, while representing important progress in environmental protection, often reflect and reinforce the anthropocentric assumptions underlying non-radical environmentalism, limiting their effectiveness in addressing more fundamental environmental concerns.

2.1.4.3 Ecocentric Philosophy and Radical Environmentalism

The evolution of environmental thought has witnessed parallel yet divergent developmental trajectories: while non-radical environmental perspectives emerged within existing societal frameworks, radical environmentalist ideas developed as a fundamental challenge to prevailing paradigms. These approaches, despite their philosophical opposition, frequently converge in concrete resistance against industrial threats. Such practical collaborations manifest in joint opposition to destructive development projects, campaigns against industrial pollution, coordinated responses to resource exploitation, and collective efforts to preserve wilderness areas. However, beyond these tactical alignments, they maintain profound philosophical and political distinctions. As Ferry articulates, "The first preserves the heritage of modern humanism intact (it is in man's interest to respect the earth), while the second implies the most radical questioning of it".[91] This radical questioning posits the inherent impossibility of resolving modern industrial crises through humanistic approaches, presenting a sophisticated critique of humanism

---

90 Dobson, A. (1998). *Justice and the environment: Conceptions of environmental sustainability and theories of distributive justice* (p. 25). Oxford University Press.

91 Ferry, L. (1992). *The new ecological order* (p. 60). University of Chicago Press.

that challenges its foundational assumptions while avoiding anti-human sentiment.

Bill Devall, a key theorist of radical environmentalism, illuminates this fundamental distinction:

> There are two great streams of environmentalism in the latter half of the twentieth century. One stream is reformist, attempting to control some of the worst of the air and water pollution and inefficient land use practices in industrialised nations and to save a few of the remaining pieces of wild-lands as "designed wilderness areas." The other stream supports many of the reformist goals but is revolutionary, seeking a new metaphysics, epistemology, cosmology, and environmental ethics of the person/planet.[92]

The designation of earth-centred approaches as "radical" emerges as a logical consequence in a world where anthropocentric dominion has persisted for millennia. This historical context, where anthropocentric values have shaped institutional structures, educational systems, economic models, and social relationships, explains why even modest proposals for environmental preservation and human activity constraints struggle to gain acceptance within mainstream discourse.

Aldo Leopold's pioneering application of ecological discoveries to environmental ethics in 1940 marked a decisive shift in environmental thought. In his seminal work "A Sand County Almanac", published posthumously, Leopold identified a fundamental dichotomy in Western ethical systems, which traditionally operated in two distinct spheres: the regulation of relationships between individuals, and the governance of individual-society interactions. His innovative contribution lay in advocating for an expansive reconceptualisation of ethical boundaries to incorporate earth, water, plants, and animals into the classical ethical framework.[93]

Leopold's analysis revealed how contemporary economic systems, driven by market imperatives of profit maximisation and resource commodification, systematically alienate people from their natural environment.

---

[92] Devall, B. (1980). The Deep Ecology Movement. *Natural Resources Journal, 20*(2), 299–322.

[93] Leopold, A. (1968). Land ethic. In *A sand county almanac* (p. 204). Oxford University Press.

This estrangement is further reinforced by educational paradigms that prioritise human achievement and technological mastery over ecological understanding and environmental connection. Modern educational institutions, he argued, perpetuate this disconnection by emphasising human dominion over nature rather than fostering understanding of ecological interdependence. This combined effect of economic and educational systems constitutes the primary obstacle to developing a comprehensive environmental ethic.

Leopold's transformative vision articulated a new ethical paradigm: "In short, a land ethic changes the role of Homo sapiens from conqueror of the land-community to plain member and citizen of it. It implies respect for his fellow-members, and also respect for the community as such".[94] This reconceptualisation demanded humanity's relinquishment of presumed environmental dominion, calling instead for recognition of human membership within the broader ecological community.[95] Through "Land Ethics", Leopold developed a comprehensive bio-centric ethical system positioning individuals within an ever-expanding society of interdependent elements – earth, water, plants, and animals.[96] His framework emphasised the ethical primacy of preserving the integrity, stability, and beauty of the entire biotic community,[97] establishing foundational principles that would evolve into modern ecocentric thought.

The etymological and conceptual foundation of ecocentrism, derived from "eco" ("house" or "earth") and "centre" – literally meaning "Earth as centre",[98] transcends conventional understandings of nature-centred approaches. This philosophical orientation moves beyond simple opposition to anthropocentrism, offering instead a fundamental reconceptualisation of ecological relationships:

---

94 Leopold, A. (1968). Land ethic. In *A sand county almanac* (p. 204, para 3). Oxford University Press.

95 Leopold, A. (1968). Land ethic. In *A sand county almanac* (p. 204, para 3). Oxford University Press.

96 Leopold, A. (1968). Land ethic. In *A sand county almanac* (p. 205). Oxford University Press.

97 Leopold, A. (1968). Land ethic. In *A sand county almanac* (pp. 224–225). Oxford University Press.

98 Mylius, B. (2013). Towards the unthinkable: Earth jurisprudence and an ecocentric episteme. *Australian Journal of Legal Philosophy*, *38*, 102–122.

> Ecocentrism has no apex at which humans, or any entity, can be placed. Rather, it is a system of ecologies, networks and relationships, in which each entity relies upon and influences those around it. The question of whether it even has a centre should remain open: properly understood, the centre of "ecocentrism" is not a fixed subject, but rather an event or process.[99]

Building upon Leopold's foundations, ecocentric philosophy offers a comprehensive theoretical structure that fundamentally reexamines humanity's position within the natural world. This reconceptualisation undertakes the essential responsibility of correcting humanity's self-positioning in the natural order, abandoning traditional human-centred perspectives while establishing a new understanding of ecological relationships. The ecocentric vision systematically challenges three entrenched assumptions: human centrality in natural systems, presumed rights of dominion over other species, and the notion that superior intelligence confers rights of environmental exploitation. Proponents of this approach demonstrate how such exploitation ultimately undermines the ecological foundations of all life, including human society, creating a self-defeating cycle where human beings suffer from their own environmental degradation.

The ecocentric imperative for environmental protection emerges not from anthropocentric concerns about human welfare, but from recognition of nature's inherent value, independent of human utility. This perspective advocates for legal and social structures that prioritise environmental protection based on nature's intrinsic rights. The inherent value in natural entities stands in direct opposition to capitalist systems that reduce nature to resources for production and economic growth, demanding protection based on intrinsic worth rather than instrumental value to human society.

The theoretical richness of ecocentric thought has generated diverse yet complementary intellectual traditions, demonstrating its non-unidimensional character. Feminist interpretations illuminate power relationships in human–nature interactions, exposing how patriarchal structures contribute to environmental degradation. Socialist analyses reveal connections between environmental exploitation and economic systems of production. Entirely new theoretical movements have emerged from these intersections, creating

---

[99] Mylius, B. (2013). Towards the unthinkable: Earth jurisprudence and an ecocentric episteme. *Australian Journal of Legal Philosophy, 38*, 102–122 (p. 106).

sophisticated networks of complementary approaches. As Zimmerman observes: "Progress could be made in ending the ecological crisis by challenging anthropocentric ethical norms and extending moral considerability to non-human beings".[100] This understanding operates simultaneously across multiple dimensions, integrating theoretical insight with practical implications.[101]

The mature ecocentric worldview establishes that humans hold moral obligations toward nature equivalent to those they hold toward each other, grounded in nature's intrinsic value rather than its utility.[102] Within this philosophical orientation, reality manifests as "an intrinsically dynamic, interconnected web of relations in which there are no absolutely discrete entities and no absolute dividing lines between the living and the non-living, the animate and the inanimate, or the human and the non-human".[103] This understanding positions humans as dependent participants within a self-regulating system, neither separate from nor superior to other components.[104]

This ecological paradigm systematically challenges conventional markers of human supremacy, demonstrating how characteristics such as intelligence, rationality, language, and tool-making capability neither negate ecological interdependence nor justify environmental dominion. The analysis reveals a critical flaw in human exceptionalism by acknowledging both the existence of humans lacking these presumed virtues and non-human beings possessing them. This critique exposes what John Rodman terms the "differential imperative"[105] – the selective recognition of attributes where humans excel while systematically ignoring the unique capabilities of other life forms. Human chauvinism emerges as a self-serving construct that conveniently fails to recognise the special attributes and capacities of other species, arbitrarily selecting only those characteristics where humans demonstrate superiority.

---

100 Zimmermann, M. E., et al. (Eds.). (1998). *Environmental philosophy: From animal rights to radical ecology* (p. 3). Prentice-Hall.

101 Moore, B. L. (2008). *Ecology and literature: Ecocentric personification from antiquity to the twenty-first century* (p. 10). Palgrave Macmillan.

102 Pepper, D. (2003). *Modern environmentalism: An introduction* (p. 15). Taylor & Francis.

103 Eckersley, R. (1997). *Environmentalism and political theory: Toward an ecocentric approach* (p. 49). UCL Press.

104 Pepper, D. (2003). *Modern environmentalism: An introduction* (p. 15). Taylor & Francis.

105 Rodman, J. (1980). Paradigm change in political science. *American Behavioral Scientist, 24*, 49–78.

While anthropocentric resource conservation acknowledges ethical considerations based on prudence and ecological self-interest, its evaluation remains constrained by exclusively human metrics. Such approaches assess ecological crises solely through human impacts, fundamentally limiting their analytical scope. The ecocentric perspective transcends these constraints by considering implications for both human and non-human entities within an integrated analytical framework. As Eckersley articulates:

> In according ontological primacy to the internal relatedness of all phenomena, an ecocentric perspective adopts an "existential attitude of mutuality" in recognition of the fact that one's personal fulfillment is inextricably tied up with that of others. This is not seen as a resignation or self-sacrifice but rather as a positive affirmation of the fact of our embeddedness in ecological relationships.[106]

Ecocentric theory conceptualises relationships through multiple intersecting dimensions, encompassing not only human-non-human interactions but also human relationships across biological, social and psychological contexts, together with their connections to political, economic, and cultural institutions.[107] Within this complex web, humans function as "relatively autonomous beings who, by our purposive thought and action, help to constitute the very relations that determine who we are".[108] This theoretical orientation advances beyond both liberalism's atomistic individualism and socialism's collective understanding, offering a more comprehensive integration that recognises both individual autonomy and ecological interdependence.

Despite its fundamental critique of human chauvinism and extensive emphasis on non-human beings, ecocentric philosophy neither opposes human existence nor denies the legitimacy of human distinctiveness. The movement's central challenge targets specifically the ideology of human chauvinism rather than humanity itself. The ecocentric vision establishes that "the equal right to live and blossom is an intuitively clear and obvious value

---

[106] Eckersley, R. (1997). *Environmentalism and political theory: Toward an ecocentric approach* (p. 53). UCL Press.

[107] Eckersley, R. (1997). *Environmentalism and political theory: Toward an ecocentric approach* (p. 53, para 2). UCL Press.

[108] Eckersley, R. (1997). *Environmentalism and political theory: Toward an ecocentric approach* (p. 53, para 2). UCL Press.

axiom"[109] for all entities within the ecological community. Yet this principle operates with pragmatic awareness that "any realistic praxis necessitates some killing, exploitation, and suppression".[110] The ecocentric approach resolves this apparent tension through what Eckersley articulates as a principle of minimal interference: "When faced with a choice, however, those who adopt an ecocentric perspective will seek to choose the course that will minimize such harm and maximize the opportunity of the widest range of organisms and communities – including ourselves – to flourish in their/our own way".[111]

This sophisticated understanding acknowledges the practical challenges inherent in implementing ecocentric principles while maintaining their theoretical integrity. The framework demonstrates how environmental protection and human flourishing need not conflict when properly understood within an ecological context. This resolution of apparent tensions between human needs and environmental protection offers a practical pathway forward, suggesting how societies might fundamentally restructure their relationship with the natural world while maintaining both ecological integrity and human welfare. The ecocentric vision thus provides not merely a critique of existing systems but a constructive framework for reimagining and reconstructing human–nature relationships in more sustainable and ethically sound ways.

2.2 Constructing the Rights of Nature

2.2.1 The Ontological Status of Nature's Intrinsic Value

The construction of the rights of nature fundamentally depends on establishing their philosophical basis, practical evolution, and contemporary manifestation in legal frameworks. These three interconnected aspects – the philosophical groundwork, the transition beyond instrumental valuation, and contemporary theoretical perspectives – demonstrate the progression from theoretical foundations to practical implementation, illustrating how the

---

[109] Naess, A. (1973). The shallow and the deep, long-range ecology movement: A summary. *Inquiry, 16*(1), 95–100.

[110] Naess, A. (1973). The shallow and the deep, long-range ecology movement: A summary. *Inquiry, 16*(1), 95–100 (p. 95).

[111] Eckersley, R. (1997). *Environmentalism and political theory: Toward an ecocentric approach* (p. 7). UCL Press.

concept of nature's intrinsic value has evolved from philosophical discourse to concrete legal recognition.

2.2.1.1 Philosophical Groundwork of Inherent Worth

The discourse on rights, particularly concerning nature, necessitates a foundational understanding of intrinsic value as its basic prerequisite. This philosophical bedrock establishes the basis for recognising and attributing rights beyond the human sphere. O'Neill's framework provides particularly valuable insights due to its systematic deconstruction of value attribution in environmental ethics, offering a tripartite structure that has significantly influenced subsequent theoretical developments.[112] His analysis delineates three distinct but interconnected interpretations of intrinsic value, each contributing to our understanding of nature's inherent worth and its implications for rights attribution.

The first interpretation positions intrinsic value as synonymous with non-instrumental value, establishing nature as an end in itself rather than merely a means to human ends. This perspective finds resonance in deep ecological thought, particularly as articulated by Naess, who emphatically asserts that "the well-being of non-human life on Earth has value in itself. This value is independent of any instrumental usefulness for limited human purposes".[113] This foundational premise challenges traditional anthropocentric valuations and establishes a philosophical basis for considering nature's autonomous worth, independent of its utility to human endeavours.

The second conceptualisation focuses on intrinsic properties, which are those characteristics inherent to an entity independent of its relational qualities. This interpretation necessitates evaluating natural entities based on their inherent attributes rather than their contextual relationships or comparative uniqueness. Such an approach fundamentally shifts the valuation paradigm from comparative or relational worth to an appreciation of nature's inherent characteristics. For instance, a species' value would not be determined by its

112 O'Neill, J. (2004). *Ecology, policy, and politics: Human well-being and the natural world* (pp. 8–9). Routledge.

113 Naess, A. (1984). A defence of the deep ecology movement. *Environmental Ethics, 6*, 265–270.

uniqueness in relation to other species or its role in the ecosystem, but rather by its intrinsic properties as an autonomous entity.

The third dimension presents intrinsic value as objective value, which is perhaps the most philosophically contentious of the three interpretations. This perspective posits that value exists independently of valuers, suggesting that nature's worth would persist even in the absence of human recognition or evaluation. To illustrate this concept concretely, if humanity were to cease existing, the intrinsic value of nature would remain undiminished – a radical departure from anthropocentric value systems. However, as Pepper critically observes, this position encounters a significant philosophical challenge: the very concepts of value, worth, and rights are human constructs, inevitably attributed to nature through human agency.[114]

This philosophical tension between recognising nature's independent worthwhile acknowledging the human origin of value systems represents a crucial challenge in environmental ethics. The paradox illuminates the complexity of establishing a philosophical foundation for the rights of nature that transcends purely anthropocentric considerations while remaining coherent within human systems of thought and valuation. Yet, this theoretical framework, despite its inherent challenges, provides the necessary groundwork for advancing discussions about the rights of nature and their practical implementation in legal and policy frameworks, leading naturally to considerations of how these values manifest beyond purely theoretical constructs.

2.2.1.2 Beyond Instrumental Valuation

The transition from purely instrumental to intrinsic valuation of nature represents a fundamental paradigm shift in environmental ethics and policy. This evolution challenges traditional anthropocentric approaches by positing nature's value beyond its utility for human purposes. The deep ecology movement, particularly through Naess's foundational work, articulates this transition most explicitly, arguing that non-human life possesses inherent value entirely independent of its instrumental usefulness for limited human purposes.[115]

---

[114] Pepper, D. (2003). *Modern environmentalism: An introduction* (p. 51). Taylor & Francis.

[115] Naess, A. (1984). A defence of the deep ecology movement. *Environmental Ethics, 6*, 265–270.

This conceptual shift necessitates a radical reconsideration of how we attribute value to natural entities. The ecocentric approach, emerging from this philosophical reorientation, manifests in two significant branches: deep ecology and social ecology. Deep ecology, advocating for the intrinsic value of all living beings, emphasises the interconnectedness of ecosystems and the equal right to existence of all natural entities. Social ecology, while maintaining the core premise of value beyond instrumentality, focuses on how social structures and hierarchies influence environmental degradation. Despite their opposing arguments on methodology and primary focus, both branches contribute to the theoretical framework that challenges purely instrumental valuations of nature.[116]

However, this transition beyond instrumental valuation encounters significant philosophical and practical challenges. The fundamental paradox, as noted by Pepper, lies in the inherent human agency in value attribution.[117] Yet, unlike the theoretical impasse discussed in the philosophical groundwork, this challenge has catalysed practical developments in environmental thought and policy. The recognition of this paradox has contributed to a more nuanced understanding of how we might reconcile human agency in value attribution with the recognition of nature's independent worth.

The progression from purely instrumental valuation to a more complex understanding of intrinsic value signifies a crucial development in environmental ethics, one that acknowledges both the limitations of human perspective and the necessity of moving beyond purely utilitarian approaches to nature. This evolution in understanding has fostered the development of more sophisticated environmental protection frameworks that attempt to balance human needs with recognition of nature's inherent worth.

This conceptual evolution has profound implications for how we approach environmental protection and policymaking. Moving beyond instrumental valuation requires not only philosophical recognition but also practical implementation through legal and policy frameworks. The shift represents a fundamental change in how human societies conceptualise their relationship

---

[116] Emmenegger, S., & Tschentscher, A. (1994). Taking nature's rights seriously: The long way to biocentrism in environmental law. *Georgetown International Environmental Law Review, 6*(3), 545–742.

[117] Pepper, D. (2003). *Modern environmentalism: An introduction* (p. 51). Taylor & Francis.

with nature, moving from a paradigm of dominion and utility to one of respect and recognition of inherent worth. This transformation in perspective sets the stage for examining how these theoretical developments have manifested in contemporary environmental governance and law.

2.2.1.3 Contemporary Theoretical Perspectives

The evolution of nature's intrinsic value from philosophical discourse to practical implementation is most evidently manifested in contemporary environmental instruments and legal frameworks. This transition represents a significant paradigm shift in how nature's value is recognised and protected at both international and national levels. While the theoretical tensions between social ecology and deep ecology persist in academic discourse, their collective influence has contributed to the practical implementation of nature's intrinsic worth in binding legal instruments.

A watershed moment in this evolution is marked by the UN Convention on Biological Diversity (1992), which explicitly acknowledges "the intrinsic value of biological diversity and of the ecological, genetic, social, economic, scientific, educational, cultural, recreational and aesthetic values of biological diversity and its components".[118] This recognition, positioned at the forefront of a legally binding international agreement, signals a decisive shift from purely anthropocentric approaches to a more nuanced understanding that encompasses nature's inherent worth alongside its instrumental values.

Further reinforcing this paradigm shift, the World Charter for Nature (UN General Assembly 1982) makes the remarkable assertion that "every form of life is unique, warranting respect regardless of its worth to man, and, to accord other organisms such recognition, man must be guided by a moral code of action".[119] Although not legally binding, this declaration holds pivotal importance in the development of environmental law and policy. As Emmenegger and Tschentscher observe, it plays a crucial role in establishing *opinio iuris* in customary international law, thereby creating a foundation for universal recognition of nature's intrinsic value.[120]

---

[118] United Nations. (1992). *Convention on biological diversity* (Preamble, para. 1).

[119] United Nations General Assembly. (1982). *World charter for nature* (A/RES/37/7, annex).

[120] Emmenegger, S., & Tschentscher, A. (1994). Taking nature's rights seriously: The long way to biocentrism in environmental law. *Georgetown International Environmental Law Review*, *6*(3), 545–742.

The historical trajectory of environmental protection agreements reveals an evolutionary progression through three distinct phases: initially focusing on protecting present generations' interests, then expanding to consider future generations, and finally acknowledging nature's intrinsic value independent of human interests.[121] This evolution represents a fundamental shift from anthropocentric to more bio-centric approaches in environmental protection, reflecting the theoretical developments discussed in previous sections.

Significantly, the terminology employed in these instruments reflects this conceptual evolution. The preference for the term "nature" over the more anthropocentric "environment" in the World Charter for Nature exemplifies this shift in perspective. Moreover, the Charter's adoption as a solemn declaration, similar to the Universal Declaration of Human Rights, underscores the gravity with which the international community has come to view nature's intrinsic rights and value.

The acceptance of nature's intrinsic value in these contemporary frameworks signifies more than mere theoretical acknowledgement; it represents a fundamental reconstruction of the human–nature relationship. This shift moves beyond the notion of humans as sole arbiters of natural protection toward recognition of nature's inherent integrity and rights, independent of human interests. The progression from anthropocentric protection to recognition of intrinsic value thus lays the groundwork for a more comprehensive understanding of the rights of nature in contemporary environmental law and policy, bringing full circle the philosophical foundations and practical implementations discussed throughout this analysis.

2.2.2 Building a Framework for Rights

2.2.2.1 Rights-Based Approaches in Environmental Protection

Building upon our previous analysis of nature's intrinsic value and its theoretical underpinnings, the examination of rights-based approaches begins at the intersection where laws become insufficient or are not applied as they should be in the context of nature, wherein the rules of ethics become directory. But it is not accurate to burden the rules of ethics with the entire social and

---

[121] Emmenegger, S., & Tschentscher, A. (1994). Taking nature's rights seriously: The long way to biocentrism in environmental law. *Georgetown International Environmental Law Review*, *6*(3), 545–742 (p. 571).

global issues of nature. It is necessary to understand what these rules are at first, and then to adopt these to the legislative platforms systematically. In this sense, it is seen that these new theoretical debates are essential to establish a new system of law.

The progression from ethical recognition to legal protection represents a crucial pattern in rights development. Moral rights determine the ethical behaviour, but they are not subject to any obligation of recognition by the governments. For instance, even though it was accepted by the majority for a long time, South African black people's moral rights are violated systematically, due to their repudiation by law. "Legal rights, in contract, are enshrined in law and are thus enforceable though societal institutions".[122] Thus, during the course of history, rights have emerged via the violation of the things that people believe in the ethical sense. Likewise, the terror of World War II created the stimulus for the Universal Declaration of Human Rights.[123]

This evolutionary pattern from moral recognition to legal codification finds particular relevance in environmental protection. As mentioned above, along with the development of the awareness of the fact that nature as a whole has an intrinsic value, the idea of nature having moral rights is expanding, though being limited. This viewpoint will fulfil itself with legal rights. On this topic, Thomas Berry defends that every being has moral rights, and these rights should be legally protected.[124] Together with deepening this view and starting off by the idea in which "the concept of law was of fundamental importance for both the protection of nature and human beings"[125] the field of Earth Jurisprudence is created. This emerging field represents a crucial bridge between traditional legal frameworks and the recognition of the rights of nature, fundamentally reshaping how legal systems approach environmental protection. In this field, also the concept of rights has changed philosophically besides its extension to all of nature:

---

122 Boyd, D. R. (2017). *The rights of nature: A legal revolution that could save the world* (p. xxxii). ECW Press.

123 Boyd, D. R. (2017). *The rights of nature: A legal revolution that could save the world* (p. xxxii). ECW Press.

124 Berry, T. (1999). *The great work: Our way into the future* (p. 4). Bell Tower.

125 Burdon, P. D. (2013). The earth community and ecological jurisprudence. *Oñati Socio-Legal Series, 3*(5), 815–837.

> From an Earth-centric perspective, the myopia of a philosophy that cannot recognize the "right" of a river to flow, of a species to remain free of genetic pollution or even of the Earth to maintain its climate, beggars belief... If the term "rights" as used in our legal system is incapable of being applied to other members of the community it is simply an indication that the legal system is insufficiently developed to reflect the reality of their existence.[126]

The evolution of rights recognition follows discernible patterns across history, offering valuable insights for environmental rights development. From a practical point of view, a conclusion can be derived via considering the history and purpose of the legal rights, without going deep on the philosophical fundamentals. For instance, during a period of time, slavery and humans being properties of each other were not considered as an unethical issue. But during time, in a new understanding which started with a few people, these applications are started to be seen cruel and barbaric. Even on the era where the debates had already started, the advocates of the old system defended that slaves are inferior creatures and thus are not worth of moral consideration. Parallel to the increase in the pressure to this view and application, the advocates of slavery had to improve the standards of their behaviours. Yet this was not seen enough and the opinion of the majority evolved into considering slavery as abhorrence. Today however, the right not to be enslaved is a basic human right, beyond dispute. As in this example, when history of civil rights, women's rights, indigenous rights, LGBTQ+ rights are considered, it is clearly visible how these rights are politically powerful, beyond their symbolic powers. But it is essential to know that "they are not a magic wand that can be waved to solve problems instantly, but they are a proven means of securing progress in the way society embraces previously mistreated communities".[127]

The development of rights-based approaches to environmental protection has generated significant theoretical critique, particularly regarding the appropriateness of applying human-centred legal concepts to nature. On the other hand, the idea that the rights-based approach would be wrong is still popular. For instance, John Livingston in this context defends the idea that

---

126 Cullinan, C. (2011). A history of wild law. In P. Burdon (Ed.), *Exploring wild law: The philosophy of earth jurisprudence* (pp. 12–23). Wakefield Press.

127 Boyd, D. R. (2017). *The rights of nature: A legal revolution that could save the world* (p. xxxiii). ECW Press.

the effort to expand the liberal egalitarian ideals "anthropomorphizes the non-human world in order to include it in a human ethical code".[128] Similarly, in the "liberation of nature" viewpoint, it is defended that extending human-like rights to non-humans is not a beneficial approach, and the solution lies in the liberation of the non-human world from "the status of human resource, human product, human caricature".[129] All this studies are the contradiction of the ideas that were put forward in order to figure out a way to effectively protect nature. These critiques raise fundamental questions about the adequacy of traditional legal frameworks for environmental protection. On the other hand, the discourses about the characteristics of the systems, from the people who study it, gain importance. Regarding this topic, also John Rawls, one of the pioneers of the modern liberal theory explains how non-human beings cannot be involved into the system via the rights-based approach as follows:

> It does not seem possible to extend the contract doctrine so as to include them [i.e. creatures lacking a capacity for a sense of justice] in a natural way. A correct conception of our relations to animals and to nature would seem to depend [instead] upon a theory of the natural order and our place in it.[130]

This fundamental tension between traditional rights-based frameworks and the unique challenges of environmental protection sets the stage for examining how legal systems might evolve to better accommodate the rights of nature. The paradox of using human constructs to protect non-human entities remains central to this development, influencing both theoretical approaches and practical implementations in environmental law.

2.2.2.2 Substantive Content and Jurisdictional Scope

The delineation of the rights of nature requires both precise substantive content and clear jurisdictional parameters to enable effective legal implementation. One of the earliest advocates of the rights of nature, Christopher Stone, cxplains the vagueness in his influential book "Should Trees Have Standing?" as:

---

[128] Livingston, J. (1981). *The fallacy of wildlife conservation* (pp. 62–63). McClelland and Stewart.

[129] Rodman, J. (1977). The liberation of nature? *Inquiry, 20*, 83–145.

[130] Rawls, J. (1976). *A theory of justice* (p. 512). Oxford University Press.

> Now, to say that the natural environment should have rights is not to say anything as silly as that no one should be allowed to cut down a tree. We say human beings have rights, but – at least as of the time of this writing – they can be executed. Corporations have rights, but they cannot plead the Fifth Amendment. In *re Gault* gave 15-year-olds certain rights in juvenile proceedings, but it did not give them the right to vote. Thus, to say that the environment should have rights is not to say that it should have every right we can imagine, or even the same body of rights as human beings have. Nor is it to say that everything in the environment should have the same rights as every other thing in the environment.[131]

This foundational clarification establishes crucial boundaries for both the content and scope of environmental rights. These explanations are important to eliminate the questions like; "If nature has rights, does it mean that we have same rights with AIDS virus?" or "Can I sue a tree that cause a loss by falling on my car?" or "When the avalanche falls, will we be able to sue the mountain?", etc. In this understanding, the non-human life forms have non-symbolic and valid rights, but these are not exactly the same as those of human beings since the logical foundations of the rights differ according to the entities respective difference in nature.[132] This differentiation provides a crucial framework for determining jurisdictional boundaries. For instance, freedom of thought and speech or freedom to engage in political participation are the rights that can only be identified with human dignity and warranted only by the human characteristic, therefore they should be granted only for human beings.[133]

The substantive content of the rights of nature emerges from fundamental principles of existence, establishing the jurisdictional foundation. According to Thomas Berry, "rights originate where existence originates, that which determines existence determines rights".[134] According to this, the right that

---

[131] Stone, C. D. (2010). *Should trees have standing: Law, morality, and the environment* (pp. 3–4). Oxford University Press.

[132] Emmenegger, S., & Tschentscher, A. (1994). Taking nature's rights seriously: The long way to biocentrism in environmental law. *Georgetown International Environmental Law Review, 6*(3), 545–742.

[133] Emmenegger, S., & Tschentscher, A. (1994). Taking nature's rights seriously: The long way to biocentrism in environmental law. *Georgetown International Environmental Law Review, 6*(3), 545–742 (p. 581).

[134] Berry, T. (2006). Ten principles for jurisprudence revision. In *Evening thoughts: Reflecting on earth as sacred community* (p. 149). Sierra Club Books.

intrinsic value grants to every living being in nature is the right to existence. This right can be established via the right to survive as a species or only via an individual living being.[135] This dual approach to rights – both individual and collective – has significant implications for jurisdictional scope and enforcement mechanisms. To some extent, causality has been established with this right, the living beings' instinct to survive and their self-preservation impulse. This mentioned right includes the freedoms for a being's natural existence, such as the freedom to move, eat and procreate.[136] In the context of the rights of nature, another fundamental right that is foreseen to be legalised is the right to life without necessary suffering for all sentient species.[137] This expansion of rights protection requires careful consideration of jurisdictional frameworks and enforcement mechanisms. When it comes to the sentient beings, this right is accepted today even by the contemporary utilitarians. But when it comes to the right of nature, this right should be interpreted in a broader way. The scope of protection extends beyond mere sentience, encompassing the fundamental characteristics that define each natural entity.

The implementation of the rights of nature demands a fundamental reconceptualisation of legal jurisdictions and enforcement mechanisms. However, among all these, the rights of nature understanding includes a broader change. Because, from a geocentric worldview, it is inconceivable to maintain a philosophical stance that fails to acknowledge fundamental natural processes – such as a river's inherent need to flow, a species' right to maintain its genetic integrity, or Earth's essential capacity to regulate its climate.[138] Thomas Berry argues that the classical theory of rights should change into such a way that it includes the rights of nature, without any conflict. According to him:

---

[135] Emmenegger, S., & Tschentscher, A. (1994). Taking nature's rights seriously: The long way to biocentrism in environmental law. *Georgetown International Environmental Law Review*, *6*(3), 545–742.

[136] Emmenegger, S., & Tschentscher, A. (1994). Taking nature's rights seriously: The long way to biocentrism in environmental law. *Georgetown International Environmental Law Review*, *6*(3), 545–742 (p. 582).

[137] Emmenegger, S., & Tschentscher, A. (1994). Taking nature's rights seriously: The long way to biocentrism in environmental law. *Georgetown International Environmental Law Review*, *6*(3), 545–742 (p. 582).

[138] Cullinan, C. (2011). *Wild law: A manifesto for earth justice* (p. 97). Green Books.

> Every component of the Earth Community has three rights: The right to be, the right to habitat, and the right to fulfill its role in the ever-renewing processes of the Earth Community. All rights are species-specific and limited. Rivers have river rights. Birds have bird rights. Insects have insect rights. Humans have human rights. Difference in rights is qualitative not quantitative. The rights of an insect would be of no value to a tree or a fish.[139]

This species-specific approach provides a practical framework for determining both substantive content and jurisdictional boundaries. When we analyse the meaning behind the statement "rivers have river rights", first of all, the fundamental rights of river will be specified. A river's fundamental river right would be the right to flow.[140] "If a water body couldn't flow it wouldn't be a river, and so the capacity to flow (given sufficient water) is essential to the existence of a river".[141] Thus, from the lake's perspective, constructing too many dams on top of it in order to drain an excessive amount of water for the agriculture and the industry is an abuse of its rights, since it will cause the water level to go down significantly.

This framework demonstrates how the theoretical understanding of the rights of nature translates into specific, enforceable legal protections. The jurisdictional scope emerges from the inherent characteristics and functions of natural entities, while enforcement mechanisms must adapt to protect these rights within existing legal systems. This approach provides both the theoretical foundation and practical guidelines for implementing and enforcing the rights of nature across different jurisdictional contexts.

2.2.2.3 Dialectical Interface with Human Rights Systems

The integration of the rights of nature into existing human rights frameworks presents complex theoretical and practical challenges that require sophisticated balancing mechanisms, both procedurally and substantively. In the context of the rights of nature, even when humans are accepted to be the sole subjects of rights, the issue of competing rights occurs; such as right to development against the right to have a healthy environment. Even among

---

139 Berry, T. (2006). Ten principles for jurisprudence revision. In *Evening thoughts: Reflecting on earth as sacred community* (p. 149). Sierra Club Books.

140 Cullinan, C. (2011). *Wild law: A manifesto for earth justice* (p. 104). Green Books.

141 Cullinan, C. (2011). *Wild law: A manifesto for earth justice* (p. 104). Green Books.

humans and with the anthropocentric intentions, the protection of nature is not easy in the human rights arena. When the rights of nature are added on top of this with a new system, other competing rights will be involved. Thus, balancing interest is extremely important for creating an effective system.

This inherent tension between human and environmental rights stems from fundamental resource dependencies and requires sophisticated procedural mechanisms for resolution. The competition between humans and the environment cannot be avoidable due to its nature; since humans use natural resources not only for civilisation, but also for habitat and a source for food. Such need directly requires consumption and destruction.[142] When the rights of nature are recognised within the legal system, this "also creates the need to balance each human right against the rights of all beings instead of only against the rights of other humans".[143]

The challenge extends beyond mere rights competition to the foundational structures of modern legal systems, particularly regarding standing and representation. The modern legal system is based on the property rights. Even though it has different rules on different areas, nature is a part of this property right. Adopting the rights of nature to the existing legal system does not mean such property rights would be abolished. However, the rights of nature will attempt to defeat the absolute authority of property owner to cause significant damage to natural entities. This intention includes the property itself and other things that are dependent on it and that are influenced by it.

The implementation of these rights requires substantial modification of existing property law frameworks. According to Cullinan, adopting the rights of nature would mean that:

> Laws would have to be changed to ensure that any person who wished to convert land from its natural state into mines, houses, roads, or farms would not be authorised to do so unless he or she could justify the interference with the existing rights of natural communities on that land. Developments that threatened the right of a species to exist would not be permitted except in exceptional circumstances

---

[142] Taylor, P. W. (2011). *Respect for nature: A theory of environmental ethics* (p. 258). Princeton University Press.

[143] Cullinan, C. (2011). *The legal case for the universal declaration of the rights of mother earth*. Rights of Nature. https://therightsofnature.org/wp-content/uploads/pdfs/Legal-Case-for-Universal-Declaration-Cormac-Cullinan.pdf

(e.g. to ensure human survival). This is what it will take to conserve the biological diversity of Earth.[144]

This transformation necessitates new procedural mechanisms and consideration of scientific evidence in decision-making. The determination of "exceptional circumstances" requires careful consideration of scientific evidence, economic implications, and intergenerational equity. Furthermore, transboundary issues arise when environmental impacts cross jurisdictional boundaries, necessitating international cooperative frameworks.

The practical implications of this rights interface become particularly evident in complex cases. In the new legal system in which the rights of nature will be adopted by earth-centred approach, it would be enlightening to emphasise the consequences of the conflicting rights. The virus case provides one illustrative example: a fatal virus would have intrinsic value too in the light of the above explanations that are done through the ecocentric perspective. Intrinsic value grants that virus the right to live via this new perspective. Ergo, this causes conflicting rights with humans right to live.

Similar conflicts arise in numerous contexts requiring balanced resolution. For instance, indigenous communities' traditional land use rights often align with environmental protection but may conflict with broader development goals. The resolution of such conflicts requires consideration of both preventive and remedial approaches, alongside established principles of environmental justice.

The resolution framework must incorporate both procedural and substantive elements. These challenges are not insurmountable, but require thorough comprehension of fundamental perspectives. According to this, any interference with the rights of nature needs justified reasoning. That is, "to exterminate it is relatively right, but inseparable from an absolute wrong".[145] Thus, it does not mean that decisions will be made in favour of nature, when the rights of nature and the rights of humans have a conflict,

---

144 Cullinan, C. (2011). *The legal case for the universal declaration of the rights of mother earth* (p. 4). Rights of Nature. https://therightsofnature.org/wp-content/uploads/pdfs/Legal-Case-for-Universal-Declaration-Cormac-Cullinan.pdf

145 Weiss, P. (1950). *Man's freedom* (p. 257). Yale University Press.

but instead, "the rights of nature approach offers a new potential for jurisprudential argumentation".[146]

2.2.3 Legal Recognition in Practice

The evolution of the rights of nature in legal systems represents a fundamental paradigm shift in jurisprudential thought, transitioning from purely anthropocentric frameworks to the recognition of nature as an autonomous rights-bearing entity. This transformation manifested through judicial precedents, constitutional innovations, and legislative developments that collectively establish a new legal philosophy of environmental protection.

2.2.3.1 Foundational Developments in Rights Recognition

The legal recognition of the rights of nature emerged through a gradual, yet transformative series of judicial and legislative developments. The watershed moment in this jurisprudential evolution came in 1972 with Christopher Stone's seminal article "Should Trees Have Standing?" which proved pivotal in the case of *Sierra Club v. Morton* (colloquially known as *Mineral King v. Morton*).[147] While the majority of the nine justices ruled against granting standing to King Valley, citing insufficient evidence of direct impact on Sierra Club members, Justice Douglas's dissenting opinion established a revolutionary legal framework that would influence environmental jurisprudence for decades. His argument that "inanimate objects are sometimes parties in litigation" drew compelling parallels between established legal fictions, such as maritime law's treatment of ships, and the potential for natural entities like "valleys, alpine meadows, rivers, lakes, estuaries, beaches, ridges, groves of trees, swampland, or even air" to possess legal standing to protect themselves from "the destructive pressures of modern technology and modern life". Douglas's opinion particularly emphasised the conception of a river as "the living symbol of all the life it sustains or nourishes", representing an entire ecological unit worthy of legal recognition.[148]

---

[146] Emmenegger, S., & Tschentscher, A. (1994). Taking nature's rights seriously: The long way to biocentrism in environmental law. *Georgetown International Environmental Law Review, 6*(3), 545–742.

[147] Boyd, D. R. (2017). *The rights of nature: A legal revolution that could save the world* (pp. 102–108). ECW Press.

[148] *Sierra Club v. Morton*, 405 U.S. 727 (1972).

This reasoned foundation catalysed significant advances in animal rights recognition across multiple jurisdictions, establishing precedents for nature's legal personhood. A landmark case emerged in Argentina's jurisprudence, where in *Re: Cecilia*, the court mandated the release of a chimpanzee from zoo captivity, explicitly recognising her inherent rights and establishing a crucial precedent for animal personhood.[149] This judicial recognition was further strengthened when Colombia's Supreme Court granted equivalent protection to an Andean Bear, formally acknowledging its status as a sentient being deserving of legal protection.[150] In the significant case of *Aamir Maroof Akhtar v. Federation of Pakistan*, the Supreme Court demonstrated how traditional values could substantiate environmental protection by prohibiting trophy hunting of the Houbara Bustard, grounding their decision in Koranic teachings and establishing a bridge between religious values and environmental rights.[151] Germany advanced this evolution by taking an even more comprehensive approach, extending constitutional protections to both domestic and wild animals, including the broader ecosystems that support them, thereby establishing a holistic framework for natural rights.[152] Ecuador demonstrated the practical application of these principles by implementing strict sanctions against shark hunters, emphasising the government's fundamental duty to protect both human and natural rights, thus bridging the gap between theoretical rights and practical enforcement.[153]

2.2.3.2 Constitutional and Legislative Integration

The integration of the rights of nature into constitutional frameworks signifies a crucial evolution beyond case-specific judicial recognition, representing

149 *Third Court of Guarantees, Mendoza, Argentina*, File No. P-72.254/15 (2016). (A. M. Hernandez, Trans.). https://www.nonhumanrights.org/content/uploads/Chimpanzee-Cecilia_translation-FINAL-for-website-2.pdf

150 *Supreme Court of Colombia, Civil Cassation Chamber*, Case of Luis Domingo Gomez Maldonado, AHC4806-2017 (2017). (J. Salcedo, Trans.). https://www.nonhumanrights.org/content/uploads/Translation-Chucho-Decision-Translation-Javier-Salcedo.pdf

151 *Aamir Maroof Akhtar v. Federation of Pakistan & Others*, Constitutional Petition No. 38 (2015).

152 *Grundgesetz* [Basic Law for the Federal Republic of Germany], Art. 20-A (Germany). https://www.gesetze-im-internet.de/englisch_gg/.

153 Echevarria, H. (2017). When sharks have lawyers. *CNH Tours*. https://www.cnhtours.com/news/2017/9/13/when-sharks-have-lawyers/.

a systematic institutionalisation of nature's legal personhood. Bolivia's constitution, despite its emphasis on industrialisation and development, established through Article 34 a revolutionary provision that "Any person, in his own right or on behalf of a collective, is authorised to take legal action in defence of environmental rights, without prejudice to the obligation of public institutions to act on their own in the face of attacks on the environment".[154] This provision marks a departure from traditional protections, establishing nature as a subject rather than object of law.

Ecuador's Constitution stands as the most progressive model globally, incorporating indigenous *buen vivir*[155] principles to balance development with ecological preservation. Unlike Bolivia's limited reference to "natural resources", Ecuador recognises nature (*Pacha Mama*) as an autonomous entity. Article 10 declares "nature shall be the subject of those rights that the Constitution recognizes for it",[156] reconceptualising legal personhood.

The Constitution's seventh chapter comprehensively delineates these rights through Articles 71–74, creating a sophisticated framework for nature's legal protection. Article 71 establishes that "Nature, or *Pacha Mama*, where life is reproduced and occurs, has the right to integral respect for its existence and for the maintenance and regeneration of its life cycles, structure, functions and evolutionary processes".[157] This article transcends traditional environmental

---

154 *Constitution of Bolivia*, Art. 34 (2009).

155 Balch, O. (2013, February 4). Buen vivir: The social philosophy inspiring movements in South America. *The Guardian*. https://www.theguardian.com/sustainable-business/blog/buen-vivir-philosophy-south-america-eduardo-gudynas.

156 According to Article 10 of Ecuador's Constitution, "Persons, communities, peoples, nations and communities are bearers of rights and shall enjoy the rights guaranteed to them in the Constitution and in international instruments.

Nature shall be the subject of those rights that the Constitution recognizes for it." (*Constitution of Ecuador*, Art.10, 2008).

157 According to Article 71 of Ecuador's Constitution, "Nature, or Pacha Mama, where life is reproduced and occurs, has the right to integral respect for its existence and for the maintenance and regeneration of its life cycles, structure, functions and evolutionary processes.

All persons, communities, peoples and nations can call upon public authorities to enforce the rights of nature. To enforce and interpret these rights, the principles set forth in the Constitution shall be observed, as appropriate.

The State shall give incentives to natural persons and legal entities and to communities to protect nature and to promote respect for all the elements comprising an ecosystem." (*Constitution of Ecuador*, Art. 71, 2008).

protection by empowering all persons, communities, peoples, and nations to enforce the rights of nature through public authorities, while simultaneously mandating state incentives for nature's protection.

Article 72 establishes nature's autonomous "right to be restored", independent of anthropocentric obligations to compensate affected communities.[158] For severe environmental impacts, including those arising from non-renewable resource exploitation, the State must establish effective restoration mechanisms and mitigate harmful consequences. Article 73 institutes preventive and restrictive measures against species extinction, ecosystem destruction, and natural cycle alterations, while prohibiting genetic asset alterations through introduced organisms.[159] Article 74 achieves a balance between ecological protection and human needs by guaranteeing communities the right to benefit from the environment while maintaining state regulation of environmental services.[160]

This approach transcends traditional third-generation rights that justified protection solely through human benefit calculations. It legitimises non-human entities as legal subjects, creates binding obligations for biodiversity preservation, and establishes novel jurisprudential principles. These innovations have influenced global developments, with similar protections

---

158 According to Article 72 of Ecuador's Constitution, "Nature has the right to be restored. This restoration shall be apart from the obligation of the State and natural persons or legal entities to compensate individuals and communities that depend on affected natural systems.

In those cases of severe or permanent environmental impact, including those caused by the exploitation of non-renewable natural resources, the State shall establish the most effective mechanisms to achieve the restoration and shall adopt adequate measures to eliminate or mitigate harmful environmental consequences." (*Constitution of Ecuador*, Art. 72, 2008).

159 According to Article 73 of Ecuador's Constitution, "The State shall apply preventive and restrictive measures on activities that might lead to the extinction of species, the destruction of ecosystems and the permanent alteration of natural cycles.

The introduction of organisms and organic and inorganic material that might definitively alter the nation's genetic assets is forbidden." (*Constitution of Ecuador*, Art. 73, 2008).

160 According to Article 74 of Ecuador's Constitution, "Persons, communities, peoples, and nations shall have the right to benefit from the environment and the natural wealth enabling them to enjoy the good way of living.

Environmental services shall not be subject to appropriation; their production, delivery, use and development shall be regulated by the State." (*Constitution of Ecuador*, Art. 74, 2008).

adopted in New Zealand, Bolivia, and numerous American communities.[161] The efficacy of these provisions depends on their systematic implementation through legislative and judicial mechanisms.

2.2.3.3 Judicial Innovation and Interpretation

Following the constitutional recognition of the rights of nature, courts began developing interpretative approaches to extend legal personhood to natural entities. The evolution of river rights exemplifies this judicial innovation in environmental jurisprudence. The *Loja-Villacamba* River in Ecuador[162] and the Whanganui River in New Zealand[163] received explicit legal recognition, establishing foundational precedents for protecting waterways as autonomous rights-bearing entities. The Colombian constitutional court further advanced this jurisprudential framework by affirming the Atrato River's intrinsic right to exist,[164] expanding the conception of natural entities as legal persons.

India's Uttarakhand high court made particularly sweeping declarations regarding the Ganges and Yamuna Rivers, demonstrating the potential scope of judicial interpretation in environmental rights. The court's landmark ruling that "the glaciers, including Gangotri & Yamunotri, rivers, streams, rivulets, lakes, air, meadows, dates, jungles, forests, wetlands, grasslands, springs and waterfalls" possess "the status of a legal person, with all corresponding rights...of a living person, in order to preserve and conserve them"[165] represents a comprehensive judicial articulation of nature's legal personhood. This ruling exemplifies the capacity of courts to broadly interpret and apply the rights of nature within existing legal frameworks, establishing a dynamic relationship between constitutional provisions and judicial interpretation.

These judicial developments, while groundbreaking, face fundamental challenges in practical implementation. The effectiveness of these legal protections depends on their integration into existing legislative enforcement

---

161 Boyd, D. R. (2017). *The rights of nature: A legal revolution that could save the world* (p. 223). ECW Press.

162 *Provincial Court of Loja*, Case No. 11121–2011-0010 (2011).

163 *Te Awa Tupua (Whanganui River Claims Settlement) Act 2017*, Public Act No. 7 (N.Z.). http://www.legislation.govt.nz/act/public/2017/0007/latest/whole.html.

164 *Colombian Constitutional Court*, Ruling T-622, Expediente T-5.016.242 (2016). https://justiciaambientalcolombia.org/2017/05/07/sentencia-rio-atrato/.

165 *Lalit Miglani v. State of Uttarakhand*, Writ Petition (PIL) No. 140 (India 2015).

systems and everyday practice. The transition from theoretical rights to tangible protection requires a sophisticated synthesis of ongoing judicial innovation, consistent enforcement mechanisms, and sustained commitment from both state institutions and civil society. This necessitates the development of new legal methodologies and enforcement paradigms that can effectively translate recognition into practical protection.

The evolution of the rights of nature through judicial interpretation demonstrates the vital relationship between constitutional provisions and their practical application. Courts have increasingly moved beyond traditional anthropocentric interpretations to recognise the inherent rights of natural entities, establishing a new jurisprudential framework that challenges conventional legal paradigms. However, the full realisation of these rights requires continued development of both theoretical frameworks and practical implementation mechanisms, ensuring that legal recognition translates into effective environmental protection.

Rights of Nature in International Law: Evolution and Challenges

3.1 Transnational Environmental Challenges and the Need for International Protection

Even with the anthropocentric approach, environmental problems are transnational and complex, with a structure that inherently defies national borders and jurisdictional boundaries. Today, it stands as a widely accepted and thoroughly documented fact that neither air, water and soil pollution nor climate change can be overcome with solely national solutions in our interconnected world. For this compelling reason, numerous international environmental conventions, institutions, and international organisations are now seeking comprehensive solutions to environmental problems in the international arena, recognising the global nature of these challenges. When the recognition of the rights of nature is taken into consideration, it will be seen that it is necessary to take place in the international law because of the necessity of international protection of nature like in the understanding of traditional environmental law as well as the ecocentric point of view already theoretically considering nature as a whole system of interconnected elements.

According to the ecocentric perspective; as human beings are not the proprietors of nature, the states should not have unlimited, lawless and infinite possession of the natural beings within their borders – a principle that challenges traditional concepts of state sovereignty. To regulate this complex relationship within the framework of certain ethical rules and established principles, the rights of nature must be protected by international law through comprehensive mechanisms. In addition, the protection of the rights of nature at the international level and the development of principles and standards compatible with this understanding would provide a paragon and essential framework for local and national legislation development and implementation. Obviously, it is a predictable fact that it will be difficult to break through centuries-old rooted understanding that has shaped legal and political systems worldwide. As this is internationally recognised, those who work and struggle persistently in isolated national jurisdictions for recognition of the rights of nature will benefit substantially in terms of their work and pace of progress towards environmental protection. A good example in the international arena leads countries to devote their scarce resources on implementation of that acknowledged standards, demonstrating the practical impact of international frameworks.

In addition to this fundamental aspect, it is a facilitator of effective protection in the countries, as more people are aware of these rights in the world and their significance for environmental preservation. "The more people who are aware of the rights of nature and the possibility of appealing to the justice system to remedy violations of those rights, the more jurisprudence will be developed in this area".[166] The establishment of various specialised institutions for the recognition and enforcement of these rights by international law will pave the way for local development by raising awareness of the whole world, even if taken first by some countries, creating a cascade effect of environmental consciousness and legal protection mechanisms.

"International law instruments already regulate directly the protection of endangered species, habitat protection, and biological diversity. International law thereby pays attention to collective goods, mainly for anthropocentric reasons".[167] However, by courtesy of sovereignty, countries can do what they want within their own territory, often prioritising economic interests over environmental concerns. If they want, they can destroy their forests, their habitats, their animals, their mines; and yet they do not have to account for any external authority despite the global implications of their actions. Deforestation, which takes place in the wake of the actions of a country,

---

[166] Suárez, S. (2013). Defending nature: Challenges and obstacles in defending the rights of nature case study of the Vilcabamba River (p. 12). Friedrich-Ebert-Stiftung Latin American Institute for Social Research.

[167] Peters, A. (2017). Introduction to symposium on global animal law (Part I): Animals matter in international law and international law matters for animals. *American Journal of International Law Unbound, 111*, 252–256.

actually affects other countries even if they are not directly neighbouring to the land, demonstrating the interconnected nature of environmental systems. All these effects are interdependent, but it is very difficult to prove through current scientific and legal frameworks.[168] From the perspective of a country, what can be done to correct the actions of another country is very limited and often ineffective: international organisations can try to convince the leaders of the country by influencing them through diplomatic channels, big funding sources can withhold support from environmentally harmful projects, "debt-for-Nature swaps" can be used by wildlife groups as alternative approaches.[169] These methods are often ineffective and vague in both implementation and outcomes. As a matter of fact, it will be seen that the system which is being implemented until today is not effective when the living ecological crisis is taken into consideration, with its mounting evidence of environmental degradation. Hence, the recognition of the rights of nature and the consideration of nature as a whole can solve these fundamental problems by providing a more comprehensive framework for environmental protection.

Although combating strategic behaviour and securing cooperation is useful in international law, it often requires a more challenging struggle to achieve a gain as compared to national law, particularly given the complexities of international relations.[170] While a definite result can be obtained with a majority rule within a democratic country, in the international arena, no country can be forced to sign an agreement because of national sovereignty principle, creating significant challenges for environmental protection. Using this fundamental principle, countries are very cautious about the international agreements, due to their interest calculations and hesitancy to take much responsibility for global environmental issues. It is therefore necessary to activate national and international law together in a coordinated and systematic approach. Because, even if it is difficult and requires sustained effort, it is vital that this issue is also supported by the international legal rules so that the relationship between nature and human beings should be put in the

---

[168] *Gaia theory*. (n.d.). http://www.gaiatheory.org/.

[169] Stone, C. D. (2010). *Should trees have standing: Law, morality, and the environment* (p. 126). Oxford University Press.

[170] Stone, C. D. (2010). *Should trees have standing: Law, morality, and the environment* (p. 127). Oxford University Press.

correct place and nature should be protected both for itself and practically for human beings, ensuring a sustainable future for all.

3.2 The Scope and Task of International Law of Nature

If the most important actor of international relations is the states, it can be said that the most important actor of international law is the treaties, establishing a fundamental parallel in international legal frameworks. Bowman notes about how success can be reached in an international affair organised by a treaty, providing essential criteria for evaluation:

> The ultimate success of any attempt to regulate an international concern by treaty is likely to be a function of at least three variables: the range, rigor and appropriateness of the treaty's substantive provisions, the effectiveness of its implementation and enforcement procedures and the level of its acceptance by states.[171]

States, like in every other issue in the international arena, "are less willing to accept instruments which contain exacting substantive obligations and which subject the domestic implementation to close scrutiny".[172] Therefore, in order to ensure an effective system for protecting the rights of nature globally, a well-prepared international agreement must be made with careful consideration of these constraints. Together with it, the importance of the enforcement system of this agreement should also be attributed as a crucial component of its effectiveness. By taking into consideration the consent-based structure of international law, it is clear that the soft-law and hard-law instruments need to be blended in a balanced and comprehensive manner. However, the regulation in this regard should be as serious as the human rights approach, given the fundamental importance of environmental protection. As a matter of fact, in the ecocentric point of view, human rights and rights of other natural entities are close if not equal to each other as Earth rights, forming an integrated system of legal protection. With this understanding, implementation of treaty provisions and effective follow-up

171 Bowman, M. J. (1989). The protection of animals under international law. *Connecticut Journal of International Law, 4*, 487–499.

172 Bowman, M. J. (1989). The protection of animals under international law. *Connecticut Journal of International Law, 4*, 487–499 (p. 494).

process are vital elements for global nature law, requiring sustained commitment and oversight.

The effective and well-established international system should range from codes and international conventions to declarations, encompassing multiple levels of legal instruments. Besides these instrumental formations, for this system to be competent, it "must involve the participation of approved, technically qualified non-governmental organizations".[173] On the issue of rights of nature, the international non-governmental organisations are more significant since they should also be responsible for defending the rights of nature globally through various mechanisms and approaches. As Oscar Horta applies the following reasoning to animals,[174] we can take a step further and apply it to nature as a whole, extending this crucial principle:

> The core idea of global justice (as applied to humans) is that the place of birth or the nationality of a person is morally irrelevant to what a human being is owed for reasons of fundamental justice. Therefore, the protection of basic interests should not be dependent on different national legislative enactments but must be guaranteed globally in a uniform way.[175]

3.3 Institutional Mechanisms for Protecting the Rights of Nature

It would be inappropriate to mention that there is a gap in national or international law, even though it is an ongoing development, that the rights of nature have not yet reached the stage of shock or disbelief, the first stage of The Kubler-Ross Change Curve.[176] This initial stage of transformation represents a critical threshold in legal evolution. Because of the radical conflicts in the existing system, a new formation in law, perhaps a systematic change is required, extending far beyond conventional legal reforms. The international

[173] Bowman, M. J. (1989). The protection of animals under international law. *Connecticut Journal of International Law, 4*, 487–499 (p. 495).

[174] Horta, O. (2013). Expanding global justice: The case for the international protection of animals. *Global Policy, 4*(4), 371–380.

[175] Peters, A. (2016). Global animal law: What it is and why we need it. *Transnational Environmental Law, 5*(1), 9–23.

[176] Rivers, E. (2007). Creative regulation: How wild law can rehabilitate governance and regulation. *Environmental Law & Management, 19*, 84–86.

system that recognises the rights of nature must contain an institutional structure composed of "*a set of principles, rules, norms and procedures*",[177] forming a comprehensive framework for environmental protection. Moreover, this structure should comprise the integrated system from global to local level, address complex dynamics of temporal and spatial scale, and change the existing primacy given to the creation of monetary richness to considerations of the ecological limitations of the economy.[178] This multifaceted requirement makes the institutional challenge massive and demands innovative approaches to governance and regulation.

At this point in the development of environmental law, one of the most significant proposals for forming an effective system has been the establishment of a World Environment Organization that will work in parallel to or in a way to challenge the workings of the World Trade Organization (WTO).[179] This proposed organisation would serve as a counterbalance to existing economic institutions. Or, if it cannot be done for economic reasons, the WTO should be reformed completely in a way that its terms of reference give priority to protection of natural resources and ecosystems.[180] As mentioned above, a very fundamental change is necessary to be able to make this legal transformation, and today, the most practical way to do this is to do it together with the United Nations, leveraging its existing global infrastructure and institutional legitimacy. This approach recognises both the urgency of environmental protection and the practical constraints of international institutional development.

3.3.1 Universal Declaration of the Rights of Mother Earth

Along with national developments, recent trends towards the ecocentric understanding from the anthropocentric one have begun to gain strength and attention in the international arena. Perhaps the most important of these

---

[177] Ivanova, M. (2010). UNEP in global environmental governance: Design, leadership, location. *Global Environmental Politics, 10*, 30–59.

[178] Garver, G. (2013). The rule of ecological law: The legal complement to degrowth economics. *Sustainability, 5*, 316–337.

[179] Baker, N. (2007). Rebalancing the system: An agenda for change. *Environmental Law & Management, 19*, 77–81.

[180] Baker, N. (2007). Rebalancing the system: An agenda for change. *Environmental Law & Management, 19*, 77–81 (p. 81).

developments was the Universal Declaration of the Rights of Mother Earth which was drafted and endorsed in the World People's Conference on Climate Change in Bolivia, Cochabamba, to be presented to the United Nations.[181] It can be said that this declaration was inspired by previous authoritarian documents such as Universal Declaration of Human Rights and Earth Charter.

As a beginning, our profound dependence and every being's interrelated and interdependence position on Earth are one of the very first emphasis in the declaration.[182] Declaration consists of three main parts. In the first part, the definition of Mother Earth and the positions of the entities on the Earth are mentioned.[183] About the rights of nature; "The Declaration makes it quite clear that if human beings are to claim inherent, inalienable human rights by virtue of the fact that we exist as humans, all beings must also have inherent, inalienable rights which arise from their existence".[184] In the second main section, the inherent rights of Mother Earth are specified; such as right to life, right to exist, right to be respected, right to regenerate its bio-capacity, and more.[185] In the third main part, obligations of human beings to Mother Earth were listed.[186] Such that, "every human being is responsible for respecting and living in harmony with Mother Earth"[187] and "human beings, all States, and all public and private institutions must establish and apply effective norms and laws for the defence, protection and conservation of the rights of Mother Earth".[188]

Currently, this international document is not binding. It is still important, however, to take this step in order to mould public opinion, to raise awareness of people from all around the world, and to increase the number of its advocates to boost political pressure to transform it into a valid document. In fact, an international document created in this way; "could prove equally valuable for the promotion of earth rights and is motivated by the

---

181 *Universal declaration of the rights of mother earth.* (2010). Rights of Nature. http://therightsofnature.org/universal-declaration/.

182 *Universal declaration of the rights of mother earth* (Preamble, paras. 1 & 4; Art. 1(2)). (n.d.). Rights of Nature.

183 *Universal declaration of the rights of mother earth* (Art. 1). (n.d.). Rights of Nature.

184 *Universal declaration of the rights of mother earth* (Art. 1(4)-(6)). (n.d.). Rights of Nature.

185 *Universal declaration of the rights of mother earth* (Art. 2). (n.d.). Rights of Nature.

186 *Universal declaration of the rights of mother earth* (Art. 3). (n.d.). Rights of Nature.

187 *Universal declaration of the rights of mother earth* (Art. 3(1)). (n.d.). Rights of Nature.

188 *Universal declaration of the rights of mother earth* (Art. 3(2)(e)). (n.d.). Rights of Nature.

idea that its ethical force is strengthened by giving it 'social recognition and an acknowledged status' even when 'no enforcement' is instituted".[189] As a matter of fact, in 2011, UN General Assembly carried out a debate on the proposed Declaration with the request of Bolivia, and since then each year the UN has adopted a resolution and hosted a continued dialogue on living in harmony with nature.[190] Therefore, permanent change is difficult, long-running but possible. In this process of change, the Universal Declaration and the other instruments formed around it are great facilitators in recognising and protecting the rights of nature afterwards. If a relatively rapid change is aimed at within the present system, it is unlikely to be carried out without a cooperation with the UN. So this journey, which started in 2011, is the right step.

3.3.2 International Rights of Nature Tribunal

Just about 5 months after the acceptance of the Universal Declaration for the Rights of Nature by acclaiming of 35,000 people, the Global Alliance for the Rights of Nature (GARN) was established by global leaders and advocates from the six continents to further galvanise the emerging movement.[191] GARN serves as a global hub with the objectives of developing and strengthening relationships, exchanging knowledge and more significantly, cooperating to advance the rights of nature's understanding and implementation.[192] Thereby, this Alliance is primarily focused on creating a jurisprudence system in which

---

[189] Burdon, P. D. (2011). Earth rights: The theory. *IUCN Academy of Environmental Law e-Journal, 1*, 1–12. http://ssrn.com/abstract=1765386.

[190] UN General Assembly noted in the resolution on Harmony with Nature in 2017; "recognizing that planet Earth and its ecosystems are our home and that 'Mother Earth' is a common expression in a number of countries and regions, noting that some countries recognize the rights of nature in the context of the promotion of sustainable development, and expressing the conviction that, in order to achieve a just balance among the economic, social and environmental needs of present and future generations, it is necessary to promote harmony with nature." United Nations General Assembly. (2016). *Harmony with nature* (A/RES/71/232, p. 2). United Nations.

[191] End Ecocide on Earth & Global Alliance for the Rights of Nature. (2015). Rights for the Earth: Towards new international standards. https://www.endecocide.org/wp-content/uploads/2015/10/3-EarthLaws-DossierUPDATE.pdf.

[192] Global Alliance for the Rights of Nature. (2010). *Statutes of the Global Alliance for the Rights of Nature*. Adopted September 5, 2010, Hacienda Manteles, Patate, Ecuador. http://therightsofnature.org/founding-statutes/.

nature is not seen as a mere property to exploit but as an entity that has a fundamental rights. GARN strives to get out of the boundaries in the existing human-centred legal system by recognising and enforcing the rights of nature; because the rights of nature movement is one of the greatest transformations that humanity can make to create a good future for all.

As a result of GARN's efforts, International Rights of Nature Tribunal was established in January 2014 and has been gathered four times respectively in Quito, Lima, Paris and Bonn. In addition to these main meetings, Conference of Parties for UN Climate Change negotiations and Regional Chambers of the International Tribunal in the United States and Australia have been held in parallel to each other. The purpose of the Tribunal is to rule the cases with the accusation of violation of the rights of nature and to propose suggestions for proper remedies and restoration of the damages. The main source of law used by the Tribunal is the Universal Declaration of the Rights of Mother Earth. In addition, the Ecuador and Bolivian Constitutions were addressed to since these countries were one of the source countries of the very first cases and the rights of nature are already recognised in their constitutions. Besides, the field of activity of the Tribunal is international, and in the all four Tribunals, cases have been examined from wide range of countries.[193]

For instance, in the last Tribunal held in Bonn in November 2017, it is decided that in all of the seven cases, the Universal Declaration of the Rights of Mother Earth is violated systematically, often together with violation of human rights. In some of these cases, the harm caused was as severe as to be considered as an ecocide. The legal system failed to provide the necessities for the prevention of the extant harm in all the cases. Mostly, the mentioned harm was caused due to activities which cannot occur without a lawful authorisation, such as deforestation and mining. It was clearly seen that such legal systems uplift the property rights and the rights of corporation above the water's, air's and ecosystems' rights to exist and to contribute to the ecological well-being of the Earth. Thus, they are worsening the climate change by hiding the destructive activities under legal legitimacy. The Tribunal stated that carbon, biological and conservation offsets and the services regarding the ecosystem are processes of financialisation.

---

193 Maloney, M. (2016). Building an Alternative Jurisprudence for the Earth: The International Rights of Nature Tribunal, *Vermont Law Review, 41*, 129–142.

They allow the privatisation of nature, making it a commodity that can be traded in the financial markets. Carbon markets are incorrect solutions, which fail to lower emissions at source.[194]

Even if the Rights of Nature Tribunal is not currently legally recognised or the decisions of the proceedings are not legally enforceable, it shows that, along with being a strong voice of the concerns of the societies, there can be a different road to solve the environmental degradation beyond the classical Western legal system. Such alternative jurisprudence "compel us to interrogate existing legal principles, practices and findings through ... a wild law lens [and] can contribute to a paradigm shift in existing legal systems".[195] Together with this effect, Tribunal is also very important in a sense that it has potential for transforming the current legislation. It is said that the decisions that are not a part of the international law and are incapable of being implemented will have "performative significance as a forum in which an alternative 'rights of nature' legal discourse can be articulated and developed".[196] At the same time, the Tribunal constitutes a good example of the institutions that will need to be established following the widespread recognition of the rights of nature in international law. In this context, the message that the Tribunal gives is that the earth-centred legal system is possible and how to protect these rights in a practical manner in international law has been well demonstrated in the four Tribunals which has taken place so far.

3.4 Enforcement Mechanisms and Legal Guardianship of the Rights of Nature

Ecocentric paradigm stands against the anthropocentric approach that prioritises the property rights in the legal systems or puts governments in the centre in the international arena and considers them the sole authority over

---

194 International Rights of Nature Tribunal. (2017). *Press release: International Rights of Nature Tribunal in Bonn finds legal systems incapable of preventing climate change and protecting nature* (p. 2). http://wecaninternational.org/uploads/cke_images/BonnRightsOfNatureTribunalFinalPR.pdf.

195 Rogers, N., & Maloney, M. (2014). The Australian wild law judgement project. *Alternative Law Journal, 39*(3), 172–175.

196 Rogers, N., & Maloney, M. (2014). The Australian wild law judgement project. *Alternative Law Journal, 39*(3), 172–175.

other beings. This fundamental opposition reflects a deeper philosophical and legal tension in contemporary environmental governance frameworks. Additionally, it aims to alter these deeply rooted institutional frameworks and philosophical perspectives that have dominated legal systems for centuries. But, the proposal for the recognition of the rights of nature is not a utopic thought that can only be applicable when the transformation occurs in the future; rather, it represents a pragmatic evolution of existing legal principles. These fundamental changes should be set as a goal and the world should be directed towards it through systematic implementation strategies and institutional development. On the other hand, the enforcement of the rights of nature on a national and global scale is possible within the current system, requiring both institutional innovation and practical adaptation of existing legal frameworks. Theoretically, as mentioned on the previous chapter, the rights of nature are not solely the extension of rights; but we can use this extension procedure to achieve some quick results in the current system while working toward more comprehensive reforms in environmental jurisprudence. According to this, the legal aspect of nature's representation is not entirely different from the conceptual topics which emerge as a result of the non-traditional right owners' representation, such as the corporations, municipalities, etc., providing established precedents for implementation and development of the rights of nature within existing legal structures.

Recognising the fact that nature has its rights, results in it being able to take a legal action in case of any violation, as in the case of individuals, through properly designated representatives and carefully structured legal mechanisms. Usually, we tend to consider the right owners as living human beings that can represent themselves, reflecting traditional juridical assumptions about legal standing and representation. Thus, the representation of nature faces the same conceptual problems that the representation of future generation also faces,[197] requiring innovative legal solutions and institutional frameworks. But today, this concern and viewpoint is abolished through evolving legal frameworks and expanding conceptions of legal personhood. In today's legal system, corporations, municipalities and even ships are granted their rights, establishing crucial precedents for the extension of legal rights to

[197] Weiss, E. B. (1992). In fairness to future generations and sustainable development. *American University International Law Review, 8*(1), 19–26.

non-human entities. "The distinction between holders of rights and non-holders of rights does not follow a pre-established scheme, but is the result of a legal convention",[198] demonstrating the flexibility inherent in legal systems to accommodate new rights-holders. Thus, the representation of the rights of nature is possible just like all other subjects of the extension, building upon established legal principles and institutional precedents.

"Representation of nature is possible by instituting a guardianship of nature, similar to the system used for children and mentally incompetent adults who are also unable to represent themselves in the legal realm".[199] This guardianship model offers a particularly apt framework for environmental protection, building upon well-established legal principles. In contemporary legal systems, the courts are allowed to appoint a legal guardian for people who are unable to defend and speak for themselves in case of possible invasions of their interests, providing a robust precedent for nature's representation. So, guardians can be appointed as a legal voice to beings, like ecosystems, animals, trees, etc. which cannot find a voice to defend themselves otherwise, ensuring comprehensive protection of natural entities through established legal mechanisms. This approach bridges the gap between traditional legal frameworks and the emerging need for environmental protection. According to Christopher Stone, these guardians "could either be drawn from existing international agencies that have the appropriate focus, such as the UN Environment Program (UNEP) and the World Meteorological Organization (WMO), or from the many non-governmental organisations (NGOs) such as Greenpeace or the World Wide Fund for Nature (WWF)".[200] Then, Stone explains how this application can come true with the following example, demonstrating practical implementation within existing institutional frameworks:

> To assure that oceanic ecosystems were being adequately accounted for, an Ocean Guardian might be designated, perhaps GESAMP (Joint Group of Experts on the

---

198 Emmenegger, S., & Tschentscher, A. (1994). Taking nature's rights seriously: The long way to biocentrism in environmental law. *Georgetown International Environmental Law Review*, *6*(3), 545–742.

199 Emmenegger, S., & Tschentscher, A. (1994). Taking nature's rights seriously: The long way to biocentrism in environmental law. *Georgetown International Environmental Law Review*, *6*(3), 545–742 (p. 587).

200 Stone, C. D. (2010). *Should trees have standing: Law, morality, and the environment* (p. 130). Oxford University Press.

> Scientific Aspects of Marine Pollution), with supplementary legal staffing. The Guardian's first chore would be to monitor. He would review ocean conditions not just to gather facts "scientifically," but with a specific eye toward assuring compliance with conventions already in place. One of the weaknesses of the 1972 London Dumping Convention (LDC) and many fishing agreements is that compliance depends almost entirely on "self-monitoring," without any independent effort to survey the activities of the signatories. The Guardian could provide it.[201]

Besides their legal functions, the guardians should be assigned with political missions to ensure comprehensive protection across multiple domains of environmental governance. Thus, when they encounter new problems, these guardians will be able to be the pioneer of new formations and multinational agreements, to express new demands on behalf of nature, in front of the international agencies,[202] functioning as both advocates and institutional innovators. Another one of their functions could be to start legal and diplomatic actions in the name of nature if they are specially entitled to intervene or counsel by the international agreements,[203] expanding their role beyond mere representation to active environmental protection. For instance, considering the possible harm to nature in the case of an international investment project, based on this authority, the guardians can take precautions, create public opinion via publishing a declaratory judgement even though the participating government choose to be neutral, demonstrating the potential for proactive environmental protection. In fact, such application is now in practice in the environmental law on the national scale, providing valuable implementation models and precedents for international adaptation. For instance, under the Superfund Legislation, the National Oceanic and Atmospheric Administration (NOAA) is designed a trustee for some natural entities and has authority to bring a legal action to recover restoration costs against any party that injures its ward,[204] establishing a practical framework for environmental guardianship. And with using this power, as a result of a

201 Stone, C. D. (2010). *Should trees have standing: Law, morality, and the environment* (p. 131). Oxford University Press.

202 Stone, C. D. (2010). *Should trees have standing: Law, morality, and the environment* (p. 131). Oxford University Press.

203 Stone, C. D. (2010). *Should trees have standing: Law, morality, and the environment* (p. 131). Oxford University Press.

204 National Oceanic and Atmospheric Administration. (n.d.). *About our agency*. https://www.noaa.gov/about-our-agency.

case in California, a chemical company named Montrose agreed to pay 64 million dollars to the Natural Resource Trustees to establish a restoration programme,[205] demonstrating the practical effectiveness of legal guardianship in achieving tangible environmental outcomes. For the representation of the rights of nature, it will be enough to extend this practice from the national to the global scale, and there are no obstacles in front of it, particularly given existing international legal frameworks and institutional mechanisms.

Implementation of the rights of nature cannot be sensibly limited to the juridical model,[206] requiring a multifaceted approach to environmental protection that encompasses both legal and social dimensions. These rights cannot correctly be identified by legislation alone, and must be supported by recognition and advocacy,[207] engaging multiple stakeholders and institutions in a coordinated effort for environmental protection. Advocacy has developed significantly in the context of nature protection, creating momentum for systemic change and institutional reform. It generates an organised upheaval and a forceful compliance through systematic engagement across multiple sectors of society and levels of governance. “This can also find expression in the monitoring of present and potential violations of these rights and avenues for social pressure to urge compliance”,[208] establishing a comprehensive framework for environmental protection. Non-governmental organisations (NGOs) have emerged as one of the most important executors of this path, serving as crucial intermediaries between legal frameworks and practical implementation while driving institutional innovation. If the necessary social transformation cannot be achieved together with the addition of the rights of nature to the legal systems via legislative regulations, and creating an international law with the soft-law rules, the attendance and its sustainability

---

[205] *United States v. Montrose Chemicals*, Dkt. No. CV 90-3122 AAH (C.D. Cal. 1990). For settlement terms and management reports, see National Oceanic and Atmospheric Administration, General Counsel for Natural Resources, Southwest Region. (n.d.). *Case documents: Montrose/PV Shelf.* http://www.darrp.noaa.gov/southwest/montrose/admin.html.

[206] Burdon, P. D. (2011). Earth rights: The theory. *IUCN Academy of Environmental Law e-Journal, 1*, 1–12. http://ssrn.com/abstract=1765386.

[207] Burdon, P. D. (2011). Earth rights: The theory. *IUCN Academy of Environmental Law e-Journal, 1*, 1-12 (p. 10).

[208] Burdon, P. D. (2011). “Earth rights: The theory.” *IUCN Academy of Environmental Law e-Journal, 1*, 1–12 (p. 11).

will not be effective, highlighting the need for comprehensive approaches to environmental protection. NGOs have become the most successful actors of this social transformation through their persistent advocacy and innovative approaches to environmental protection. They have already started to advance earth rights with public discussions, education programmes and campaigns against violations,[209] demonstrating the practical path forward for environmental protection. While legal rights and legal enforcement remain the most effective mechanisms and must be satisfied in the sense of the rights of nature, public advocacy and enforcement can be enhanced through continued development of institutional frameworks and practical implementation strategies, creating a comprehensive system for environmental protection that bridges legal, social, and institutional domains.

[209] Burdon, P. D. (2011). Earth rights: The theory. *IUCN Academy of Environmental Law e-Journal, 1*, 1–12 (p. 11).

Conclusion: Envisioning the Future of Environmental Protection

4.1 Synthesis of Philosophical and Legal Developments

The recognition of nature's intrinsic value and rights represents not merely a novel legal concept but a fundamental transformation in human understanding of our relationship with the natural world. Throughout this analysis, while these ideas aren't new, their implementation faces significant resistance from academia, practitioners, governments, and civil society. This resistance stems primarily from deeply entrenched anthropocentric beliefs that have become systematically reinforced through philosophical traditions, religious interpretations, and legal frameworks. The combination of these factors with capitalist economic systems has created an "inexorable vicious circle" that underlies our current ecological crisis.[210]

However, the rights of nature movement stands not as a "romantic utopia" but as a scientifically grounded response to environmental degradation. It builds upon established scientific understanding, including Gaia theory, climate change research, and biodiversity loss data, while acknowledging the fundamental failure of traditional environmental protection approaches. The movement's philosophical foundation rests on the recognition that humans exist as part of nature, participating in an interconnected web of existence that demands protection of all its components.

The legal evolution of the rights of nature has progressed from isolated theoretical proposals to concrete constitutional provisions and judicial decisions.

[210] Boyd, D. R. (2017). *The rights of nature: A legal revolution that could save the world* (p. 230). ECW Press.

This development reflects a crucial understanding: "human rights are meaningless and cannot be sustained if Earth has no rights. The rights to life are an empty slogan without food and water, which can only be provided by Earth".[211] This fundamental connection between human wellbeing and environmental protection provides practical justification for the rights of nature even within anthropocentric frameworks.

4.2 Critical Assessment of Contemporary Framework

The current environmental protection regime, despite decades of development, reveals significant structural limitations. Traditional approaches have failed to address fundamental ecological challenges, largely because they operate within the same anthropocentric paradigms that generated these problems. This inadequacy stems from multiple factors.

The conflict between the rights of nature and existing economic structures presents perhaps the most significant challenge. These rights fundamentally challenge "infinite economic growth, excess consumption, unconstrained globalization and free market economy". Environmental protection must address both human and non-human nature, requiring simultaneous transformation of economic, social, and legal systems.[212]

The rights of nature implementation faces particular challenges in legal and institutional frameworks. The observation that "Law does not change society in itself but it points the way"[213] highlights how legal recognition represents only the first step in a broader social transformation. This insight from the US Civil Rights movement demonstrates how legal reform can catalyse broader social change, even when facing deeply entrenched resistance.

The current framework's limitations extend beyond mere legal constraints to encompass broader social and educational challenges. The absence of an "informed public that does not consider itself existentially superior to other

---

211 Cullinan, C. (2011). *Wild law: A manifesto for earth justice* (p. 190). Green Books.

212 Boyd, D. R. (2017). *The rights of nature: A legal revolution that could save the world* (p. 230). ECW Press.

213 Rivers, E. (2007). Creative regulation: How wild law can rehabilitate governance and regulation. *Environmental Law & Management, 19*, 84–86.

beings" presents a crucial obstacle to effective implementation.[214] Successful environmental protection requires fundamental transformation of public consciousness and educational systems, not merely legal reform.

Current institutional structures also demonstrate significant inadequacy in addressing environmental challenges. The precise meaning and practical effects of the rights of nature will require extensive development through "community conversations, scholarly dialogue, public and political debates, negotiation, and, where necessary, litigation, just as all novel legal concepts evolve".[215] This evolution demands new institutional frameworks capable of facilitating these complex negotiations while protecting ecological interests.

4.3 Future Directions and Recommendations

The path forward requires comprehensive transformation across multiple domains, integrating philosophical understanding with practical implementation. Based on our analysis, several key recommendations emerge for advancing the rights of nature while addressing current systemic limitations.

First, educational reform stands as a crucial priority. As Boyd emphasises, we need "an educational system which is sensitive to this topic … together with the frequent mention of the rights of nature in various communities, and natural awareness to be an essential criterion while selecting administrators".[216] This educational transformation must extend beyond formal institutions to encompass broader public awareness and understanding.

Second, institutional development must focus on creating frameworks that can effectively represent and protect nature's interests. The restrictions imposed by the rights of nature should be carefully calibrated, focusing on preventing animal suffering, species extinction, and destruction of life-supporting ecological systems.[217] These protections must be implemented

---

[214] Boyd, D. R. (2017). *The rights of nature: A legal revolution that could save the world* (p. 231). ECW Press.

[215] Boyd, D. R. (2017). *The rights of nature: A legal revolution that could save the world* (p. 230). ECW Press.

[216] Boyd, D. R. (2017). *The rights of nature: A legal revolution that could save the world* (p. 231). ECW Press.

[217] Boyd, D. R. (2017). *The rights of nature: A legal revolution that could save the world* (p. 230). ECW Press.

through robust institutional mechanisms while maintaining flexibility for human development within ecological constraints.

Third, legal frameworks must evolve to better reflect ecological realities. While top-down legal reform alone cannot "all of a sudden solve all the problems, or change the behavioural patterns", it provides essential direction for social transformation.[218] This evolution requires careful balance between immediate practical needs and longer-term ecological imperatives.

Looking forward, the rights of nature movement offers genuine potential for creating "a world in which humans live in genuine harmony with nature".[219] While this transformation presents significant challenges, it increasingly appears not merely desirable but necessary for human survival. As Cullinan powerfully argues, human rights themselves depend fundamentally on Earth's rights, making this evolution essential for both human and ecological wellbeing.[220]

This transformation, though demanding, will occur "one way or another", with earlier implementation offering better outcomes for both human society and natural systems. Success requires integration of theoretical understanding with practical implementation, combining ambitious vision with realistic assessment of implementation challenges. The future of environmental protection thus depends on our ability to transform fundamental human–nature relationships while developing effective mechanisms for protecting ecological integrity.

---

218 Rivers, E. (2007). Creative regulation: How wild law can rehabilitate governance and regulation. *Environmental Law & Management, 19*, 84–86.

219 Boyd, D. R. (2017). *The rights of nature: A legal revolution that could save the world* (p. 232). ECW Press.

220 Cullinan, C. (2011). *Wild law: A manifesto for earth justice* (p. 190). Green Books.

Universal Declaration of Rights of Mother Earth

World People's Conference on Climate Change and the Rights of Mother Earth
Cochabamba, Bolivia
22 April 2010

Preamble

We, the peoples and nations of Earth:

considering that we are all part of Mother Earth, an indivisible, living community of interrelated and interdependent beings with a common destiny;

gratefully acknowledging that Mother Earth is the source of life, nourishment and learning and provides everything we need to live well;

recognizing that the capitalist system and all forms of depredation, exploitation, abuse and contamination have caused great destruction, degradation and disruption of Mother Earth, putting life as we know it today at risk through phenomena such as climate change;

convinced that in an interdependent living community it is not possible to recognize the rights of only human beings without causing an imbalance within Mother Earth;

affirming that to guarantee human rights it is necessary to recognize and defend the rights of Mother Earth and all beings in her and that there are existing cultures, practices and laws that do so; conscious of the urgency of taking decisive, collective action to transform structures and systems that cause climate change and other threats to Mother Earth;

proclaim this Universal Declaration of the Rights of Mother Earth, and call on the General Assembly of the United Nation to adopt it, as a common standard of achievement for all peoples and all nations of the world, and to the end that every individual and institution takes responsibility for promoting through teaching, education, and consciousness raising, respect for the rights recognized in this Declaration and ensure through prompt and progressive measures and mechanisms, national and international, their universal and effective recognition and observance among all peoples and States in the world.

Article 1. Mother Earth

(1) Mother Earth is a living being.
(2) Mother Earth is a unique, indivisible, self-regulating community of interrelated beings that sustains, contains and reproduces all beings.
(3) Each being is defined by its relationships as an integral part of Mother Earth.
(4) The inherent rights of Mother Earth are inalienable in that they arise from the same source as existence.
(5) Mother Earth and all beings are entitled to all the inherent rights recognized in this Declaration without distinction of any kind, such as may be made between organic and inorganic beings, species, origin, use to human beings, or any other status.
(6) Just as human beings have human rights, all other beings also have rights which are specific to their species or kind and appropriate for their role and function within the communities within which they exist.
(7) The rights of each being are limited by the rights of other beings and any conflict between their rights must be resolved in a way that maintains the integrity, balance and health of Mother Earth.

Article 2. Inherent Rights of Mother Earth

(1) Mother Earth and all beings of which she is composed have the following inherent rights:
  (a) the right to life and to exist;
  (b) the right to be respected;
  (c) the right to regenerate its bio-capacity and to continue its vital cycles and processes free from human disruptions;

(d) the right to maintain its identity and integrity as a distinct, self-regulating and interrelated being;
(e) the right to water as a source of life;
(f) the right to clean air;
(g) the right to integral health;
(h) the right to be free from contamination, pollution and toxic or radioactive waste;
(i) the right to not have its genetic structure modified or disrupted in a manner that threatens its integrity or vital and healthy functioning;
(j) the right to full and prompt restoration for violations of the rights recognized in this Declaration caused by human activities;

(2) Each being has the right to a place and to play its role in Mother Earth for her harmonious functioning.
(3) Every being has the right to wellbeing and to live free from torture or cruel treatment by human beings.

Article 3. Obligations of human beings to Mother Earth

(1) Every human being is responsible for respecting and living in harmony with Mother Earth.
(2) Human beings, all States, and all public and private institutions must:
(a) act in accordance with the rights and obligations recognized in this Declaration;
(b) recognize and promote the full implementation and enforcement of the rights and obligations recognized in this Declaration;
(c) promote and participate in learning, analysis, interpretation and communication about how to live in harmony with Mother Earth in accordance with this Declaration;
(d) ensure that the pursuit of human wellbeing contributes to the wellbeing of Mother Earth, now and in the future;
(e) establish and apply effective norms and laws for the defence, protection and conservation of the rights of Mother Earth;
(f) respect, protect, conserve and where necessary, restore the integrity, of the vital ecological cycles, processes and balances of Mother Earth;
(g) guarantee that the damages caused by human violations of the inherent rights recognized in this Declaration are rectified and that those responsible are held accountable for restoring the integrity and health of Mother Earth;

(h) empower human beings and institutions to defend the rights of Mother Earth and of all beings;
(i) establish precautionary and restrictive measures to prevent human activities from causing species extinction, the destruction of ecosystems or the disruption of ecological cycles;
(j) guarantee peace and eliminate nuclear, chemical and biological weapons;
(k) promote and support practices of respect for Mother Earth and all beings, in accordance with their own cultures, traditions and customs;
(l) promote economic systems that are in harmony with Mother Earth and in accordance with the rights recognized in this Declaration.

Article 4. Definitions

(1) The term "being" includes ecosystems, natural communities, species and all other natural entities which exist as part of Mother Earth.
(2) Nothing in this Declaration restricts the recognition of other inherent rights of all beings or specified beings.

The Timeline of the Rights of Nature*

1972

- Southern California Law Review publishes Christopher Stone's seminal article "Should trees have standing," establishing first legal framework for nature's rights.

1989

- Professor Roderick Nash publishes "The Rights of Nature: A History of Environmental Ethics," examining how historically right-less entities gained legal recognition.

2001

- Thomas Berry publishes "The Origin, Differentiation and Role of Rights," articulating how all Earth community members possess inherent rights.

2003

- Cormac Cullinan publishes "Wild Law: A Manifesto for Earth Justice," adding spiritual and moral dimensions to legal discourse.

2006

- Tamaqua Borough, Pennsylvania becomes first place worldwide to recognize Rights of Nature, banning toxic sewage sludge. Catalyses dozens of similar laws across U.S. states.

---

*: The content was taken from <https://celdf.org/rights/rights-of-nature/rights-nature-timeline/> and <http://therightsofnature.org/timeline/>.

2008

- Ecuador becomes first country to recognize Rights of Nature in national constitution, leading to landmark 2011 Vilcabamba River case.

2009

- UN General Assembly proclaims "International Mother Earth Day" with Bolivian President Morales' advocacy.

2010

- Bolivia hosts World People's Conference, producing Universal Declaration on Rights of Mother Earth
- First UN Secretary-General Report on Harmony with Nature published
- Global Alliance for Rights of Nature formed for worldwide advancement
- Bolivia's Legislative Assembly passes Law of Rights of Mother Earth

2011

- Nepal launches Rights of Nature campaign, leading to constitutional considerations
- Ecuador's Vilcabamba River wins first Rights of Nature lawsuit, stopping harmful highway construction

2012

- India launches campaign for Ganga River rights ("Ganga's Rights are Our Rights")
- IUCN adopts Rights of Nature in decision-making processes
- Bolivia adopts comprehensive Mother Earth law
- New Zealand recognizes Whanganui River as legal person
- UN Conference (Rio+20) mentions Rights of Nature in "The Future We Want"

2013

- European Citizen's Initiative for Rights of Nature launched, enabling citizen proposals to EU government.

2014

- First Rights of Nature state constitutional amendment proposed in Colorado
- New Zealand's Te Urewera Act grants legal recognition to former national park
- First Rights of Nature Tribunal held in Quito, presided by Vandana Shiva
- Second International Tribunal launched in Lima during COP20

2015

- Sweden's Riksdag considers commission for Rights of Nature incorporation
- Pope Francis declares environmental rights at UN
- Third International Rights of Nature Tribunal held in Paris during COP21

2016

- Green Party of England and Wales adopts Rights of Nature platform
- Ho-Chunk Nation initiates first tribal Rights of Nature constitutional amendment
- Colombia's Constitutional Court grants Rio Atrato rights and establishes joint guardianship
- San Francisco Bay-Delta Ecosystem Special Tribunal held
- First Experts' Report on Earth Jurisprudence published

2017

- New Zealand finalizes Te Awa Tupua Act for Whanganui River
- India's High Court recognizes Ganga and Yamuna Rivers as legal persons
- Lafayette, Colorado enacts first Climate Bill of Rights
- Colorado River files groundbreaking federal lawsuit for legal rights
- Rights of Nature Symposium establishes key principles at Tulane
- Fourth International Tribunal held in Bonn during COP23

2018

- Ponca Nation adopts customary law recognizing nature's rights
- Colombian Supreme Court declares Amazon "subject of rights"

Key Legal Precedents in Rights of Nature (2018–2024)

Constitutional and Legislative Developments:

Panama (2022)
Law 287 establishing Rights of Nature:

- Recognizes nature as a subject of rights
- Establishes government obligations to protect nature
- Creates enforcement mechanisms for rights violations

Mexico City (2022)
Constitutional Amendment Article 13:

- Recognizes nature as a collective entity with rights
- Establishes government as nature's guardian
- Creates specific protections for urban ecosystems

Spain (2023)
Mar Menor Law:

- First European law granting legal personhood to lagoon ecosystem
- Establishes guardianship committee
- Creates specific enforcement mechanisms

Landmark Court Decisions:

Bangladesh High Court (2019)
Flowing Rivers Case:

- Granted all rivers legal personhood
- Established National River Protection Commission
- Created precedent for ecosystem rights enforcement

Montana Youth Climate Case (2023)
Held v. Montana:

- First U.S. constitutional climate case victory
- Recognized youth's right to healthy environment
- Referenced Rights of Nature principles

Colombia Constitutional Court (2021)
Páramo Ecosystem Case:

- Extended rights recognition to highland ecosystems
- Established integrated protection framework
- Created precedent for ecosystem restoration rights

Indigenous Rights Recognition:

Ponca Nation (2020)
Rights of Nature Statute:

- Recognized inherent rights of ecosystems
- Integrated traditional ecological knowledge
- Established tribal enforcement mechanisms

Māori Water Rights (2022)
Te Mana o te Wai Framework:

- Recognized rivers as living entities
- Integrated indigenous guardianship principles
- Established co-management structures

International Developments:

UN General Assembly (2023)
Resolution A/RES/77/224:

- Acknowledged Rights of Nature principles
- Called for member state recognition
- Established reporting mechanisms

Global Alliance Tribunals (2020–2024)
Major Cases:

- Amazon Rainforest Rights Violations
- Climate Change Impacts
- Ocean Ecosystem Protection

Bibliography

Aquinas, T. (1947). *Summa theologica*. Benziger Brothers. http://www.ccel.org/ccel/aquinas/summa

Baker, N. (2007). Rebalancing the system: An agenda for change. *Environmental Law & Management, 19*, 77–81.

Balch, O. (2013, February 4). Buen vivir: The social philosophy inspiring movements in South America. *The Guardian*. https://www.theguardian.com/sustainable-business/blog/buen-vivir-philosophy-south-america-eduardo-gudynas

Bentham, J. (1948). *An introduction to the principles of morals and legislation*. Nabu Press.

Berry, T. (1999). *The great work: Our way into the future*. Bell Tower.

Berry, T. (2006). Ten principles for jurisprudence revision. In *Evening thoughts: Reflecting on earth as sacred community*. Sierra Club Books.

Bowman, M. J. (1989). The protection of animals under international law. *Connecticut Journal of International Law, 4*, 487–499.

Boyd, D. R. (2017). *The rights of nature: A legal revolution that could save the world*. ECW Press.

Burdon, P. D. (2011). Earth rights: The theory. *IUCN Academy of Environmental Law e-Journal, 1*, 1–12. http://ssrn.com/abstract=1765386

Burdon, P. D. (2013). The earth community and ecological jurisprudence. *Oñati Socio-Legal Series, 3*(5), 815–837.

Butchvarov, P. (2015). *Anthropocentrism in philosophy: Realism, antirealism, semirealism*. De Gruyter.

Cook, J. et al. (2013). Quantifying the consensus on anthropogenic global warming in the scientific literature. *Environmental Research Letters, 8*(2), 024024.

Cullinan, C. (2011). A history of wild law. In P. Burdon (Ed.), *Exploring wild law: The philosophy of earth jurisprudence* (pp. 12–23). Wakefield Press.

Cullinan, C. (2011). *The legal case for the universal declaration of the rights of mother earth*. Rights of Nature. https://therightsofnature.org/wp-content/uploads/pdfs/Legal-Case-for-Universal-Declaration-Cormac-Cullinan.pdf.

Cullinan, C. (2011). *Wild law: A manifesto for earth justice*. Green Books.

Dauvergne, P. (2009). *The A to Z of environmentalism*. Scarecrow Press.

Demos, T. J. (2015). Rights of nature: Art and ecology in the Americas. In *Rights of nature* [Exhibition catalog]. Nottingham Contemporary.

Devall, B. (1980). The Deep Ecology Movement. *Natural Resources Journal, 20*(2), 299–322.

Dobson, A. (1998). *Justice and the environment: Conceptions of environmental sustainability and theories of distributive justice*. Oxford University Press.

Dobson, A. (2007) *Green Political Thought*, Routledge Taylor & Francis Group.

Driver, J. (2014). The history of utilitarianism. In E. N. Zalta (Ed.), *The Stanford encyclopedia of philosophy* (Winter 2014 ed.). https://plato.stanford.edu/archives/win2014/entries/utilitarianism-history/

Eaton, R. M. (1927). Letter to Henry More. In *Descartes selections*. Scribner.

Echevarria, H. (2017). When sharks have lawyers. *CNH Tours*. https://www.cnhtours.com/news/2017/9/13/when-sharks-have-lawyers/

Eckersley, R. (1997). *Environmentalism and political theory: Toward an ecocentric approach*. UCL Press.

Elliot, R. (1994). Ecology and the ethics of environmental restoration. In R. Attfield & A. Belsey (Eds.), *Philosophy and the natural environment* (Royal Institute of Philosophy Supplement 36, pp. 31–43). Cambridge University Press.

Elliott, L. (2018). Environmentalism. In *Encyclopædia Britannica*. https://www.britannica.com/topic/environmentalism

Emmeneger, S., & Tschentscher, A. (1994). Taking nature's rights seriously: The long way to biocentrism in environmental law. *Georgetown International Environmental Law Review, 6*(3), 545–742.

Ferry, L. (1992). *The new ecological order.* University of Chicago Press.

Garver, G. (2013). The rule of ecological law: The legal complement to degrowth economics. *Sustainability, 5*, 316–337.

Giddens, A. (1990). *The consequences of modernity*. Polity Press.

Gillespie, A. (2014). *International environmental law, policy, and ethics*. Oxford University Press.

Hanna, S., Folke, C., & Maler, K. G. (Eds.). (1996). *Rights to nature: Ecological, economic, cultural, and political principles of institutions for the environment*. Island Press.

Hoch, D. (1987). Environmental ethics and nonhuman interests: A challenge to anthropocentric license. *Gonzaga Law Review, 23*, 331–347.

Horta, O. (2013). Expanding global justice: The case for the international protection of animals. *Global Policy, 4*(4), 371–380.

Hurrell, A. (2006). The state. In A. Dobson & R. Eckersley (Eds.), *Political theory and the ecological challenge*. Cambridge University Press.

Ivanova, M. (2010). UNEP in global environmental governance: Design, leadership, location. *Global Environmental Politics, 10*, 30–59.

Kant, I. (2007). *Critique of judgement* (J. C. Meredith, Trans.; N. Walker, Ed.). Oxford University Press.

Kricher, J. (2009). *The balance of nature: Ecology's enduring myth*. Princeton University Press.

Lazarus, R. J. (2004). *The making of environmental law*. University of Chicago Press.

Leopold, A. (1968). Land ethic. In *A sand county almanac*. Oxford University Press.

Livingston, J. (1981). The fallacy of wildlife conservation. McClelland and Stewart.

Locke, J. (1936). *Two Treatises of Civil Government*. Dent.

Locke, J. (1998). *An Essay Concerning Human Understanding*. Penguin.

Machan, T. R. (2004). *Putting humans first: Why we are nature's favorite*. Rowman & Littlefield.

Maloney, M. (2016). Building an Alternative Jurisprudence for the Earth: The International Rights of Nature Tribunal, *Vermont Law Review*, Vol:41, pp. 129–142.

McNally, R., & Wheale, P. (1994). Environmental and medical bioethics in late modernity: Anthony Giddens, genetic engineering and the post-modern state. In R. Attfield & A. Belsey (Eds.), *Philosophy and the natural environment*. Cambridge University Press.

Midgley, M. (1994). The end of anthropocentricism? In R. Attfield (Ed.), *Philosophy and the natural environment*. Cambridge University Press.

Milam, R. (2013). Rights of nature and our responsibilities as earth community. *The Rights of Nature*. https://www.therightsofnature.org.

Mill, J. S. (1985). Utilitarianism. In J. M. Robson (Ed.), *The collected works of John Stuart Mill, Volume X: Essays on ethics, religion, and society*. University of Toronto Press (Original work published 1861).

Mill, J. S. (n.d.). Nature. In L. J. Matz (Ed.), *Three essays on religio*. Broadview Editions.

Moore, B. L. (2008). *Ecology and literature: Ecocentric personification from antiquity to the twenty-first century*. Palgrave Macmillan.

Moore, B. L. (2017). *Ecological literature and the critique of anthropocentrism*. Palgrave Macmillan.

Murray, J. (2014). Earth jurisprudence, wild law, emergent law: The emerging field of ecology and law – Part 1. *Liverpool Law Review, 35*, 215–231. https://doi.org/10.1007/s10991-014-9148-1.

Mylius, B. (2013). Towards the unthinkable: Earth jurisprudence and an ecocentric episteme. *Australian Journal of Legal Philosophy, 38*, 102–122.

Naess, A. (1973). The shallow and the deep, long-range ecology movement: A summary. *Inquiry, 16*(1), 95–100.

Naess, A. (1984). A defence of the deep ecology movement. *Environmental Ethics, 6*, 265–270.

Nash, R. (1989). *The rights of nature: A history of environmental ethics*. University of Wisconsin Press.

O'Neill, J. (2004). Ecology, policy, and politics: Human well-being and the natural world. Routledge.

Pepper, D. (2003). *Modern environmentalism: An introduction*. Taylor & Francis.

Peters, A. (2016). Global animal law: What it is and why we need it. *Transnational Environmental Law, 5*(1), 9–23.

Peters, A. (2017). Introduction to symposium on global animal law (Part I): Animals matter in international law and international law matters for animals. *American Journal of International Law Unbound, 111*, 252–256.

Peterson Del Mar, D. (2006). *Environmentalism*. Pearson Longman.

Pūraitė, A. (2012). Origins of environmental regulation. *Jurisprudencija, 19*(2), 657–674.

Rawls, J. (1976). *A theory of justice*. Oxford University Press.

Rivers, E. (2007). Creative regulation: How wild law can rehabilitate governance and regulation. *Environmental Law & Management, 19*, 84–86.

Rodman, J. (1977). The liberation of nature? *Inquiry, 20*, 83–145.

Rodman, J. (1980). Paradigm change in political science. *American Behavioral Scientist, 24*, 49–78.

Rogers, N., & Maloney, M. (2014). The Australian wild law judgement project. *Alternative Law Journal, 39*(3), 172–175.

Russell, B. (2009). My mental development. In R. Egner & L. Denonn (Eds.), *The basic writings of Bertrand Russell*. Routledge.

Schwartzman, D. (1999). *Life, temperature, and the earth: The self-organizing biosphere*. Columbia University Press.

Singer, P. (1993). *Practical ethics* (2nd ed.). Cambridge University Press.

Sorabji, R. (1993). *Animal minds and human morals: The origins of the western debate*. Cornell University Press.

Steiner, G. (2010). *Anthropocentrism and its discontents: The moral status of animals in the history of western philosophy*. University of Pittsburgh Press.

Stone, C. D. (2010). *Should trees have standing: Law, morality, and the environment*. Oxford University Press.

Suárez, S. (2013). Defending nature: Challenges and obstacles in defending the rights of nature case study of the Vilcabamba River (p. 12). Friedrich-Ebert-Stiftung Latin American Institute for Social Research.

Tarlock, A. D. (2009). History of environmental law. In A. D. Tarlock & J. C. Dembach (Eds.), *Environmental laws and their enforcement* (Vol. 1, pp. 41–65). Encyclopedia of Life Support Systems.

Taylor, P. W. (2011). *Respect for nature: A theory of environmental ethics*. Princeton University Press.

The Holy Bible: New International Version. (2011). Zondervan.

Weiss, E. B. (1992). In fairness to future generations and sustainable development. *American University International Law Review, 8*(1), 19–26.

Weiss, P. (1950). *Man's freedom*. Yale University Press.

Welch, C. (2018, January 4). Climate change is suffocating large parts of the ocean. *National Geographic*. https://news.nationalgeographic.com/2018/01/climate-change-suffocating-low-oxygen-zones-ocean/

Wissenburg, M. (2006). Liberalism. In A. Dobson & R. Eckersley (Eds.), *Political theory and the ecological challenge*. Cambridge University Press.

Zimmermann, M. E., et al. (Eds.). (1998). *Environmental philosophy: From animal rights to radical ecology*. Prentice-Hall.

Legal Documents

Aamir Maroof Akhtar v. Federation of Pakistan & Others, Constitutional Petition No. 38 (2015).

Constitution of Bolivia. (2009).

Colombian Constitutional Court, Ruling T-622, Expediente T-5.016.242 (2016). https://justiciaambientalcolombia.org/2017/05/07/sentencia-rio-atrato/

Ecuador's Constitution of 2008.

Grundgesetz [Basic Law for the Federal Republic of Germany], Art. 20-A (Germany). https://www.gesetze-im-internet.de/englisch_gg/

Lalit Miglani v. State of Uttarakhand, Writ Petition (PIL) No. 140 (India 2015).

Provincial Court of Loja, Case No. 11121-2011-0010 (2011). (Ecuador).

Sierra Club v. Morton, 405 U.S. 727 (1972).

Supreme Court of Colombia, Civil Cassation Chamber, Case of Luis Domingo Gomez Maldonado, AHC4806-2017 (2017). (J. Salcedo, Trans.). https://www.nonhumanrights.org/content/uploads/Translation-Chucho-Decision-Translation-Javier-Salcedo.pdf

Te Awa Tupua (Whanganui River Claims Settlement) Act 2017, Public Act No. 7 (N.Z.). http://www.legislation.govt.nz/act/public/2017/0007/latest/whole.html

Third Court of Guarantees, Mendoza, Argentina, File No. P-72.254/15 (2016). (A. M. Hernandez, Trans.). https://www.nonhumanrights.org/content/uploads/Chimpanzee-Cecilia_translation-FINAL-for-website-2.pdf

United States v. Montrose Chemicals, Dkt. No. CV 90-3122 AAH (C.D. Cal. 1990). For settlement terms can and management reports, see National Oceanic and Atmospheric Administration, General Counsel for Natural Resources, Southwest Region. (n.d.). *Case documents: Montrose/PV Shelf.* http://www.darrp.noaa.gov/southwest/montrose/admin.html

Institutional Documents

Council of the European Communities. (1973). *Declaration of the council of the european communities on the program of action of the european community on the environment* (73/C 112/01).

International Rights of Nature Tribunal. (2017). *Press release: International Rights of Nature Tribunal in Bonn finds legal systems incapable of preventing climate change and protecting nature.* http://wecaninternational.org/uploads/cke_images/BonnRightsOfNatureTribunalFinalPR.pdf

United Nations General Assembly. (1982). *World charter for nature* (A/RES/37/7).

United Nations General Assembly. (2016). *Harmony with nature* (A/RES/71/232). United Nations.

United Nations. (1972). *Report of the United Nations conference on the human environment* (A/CONF.48/14/Rev.1).

United Nations. (1986). *Declaration on the right to development* (A/RES/41/128).

United Nations. (1992). *Convention on biological diversity.*

United Nations. (1992). *Rio declaration on environment and development* (A/CONF.151/26).

Universal declaration of the rights of mother earth. (2010). Rights of Nature. http://therightsofnature.org/universal-declaration/

End Ecocide on Earth & Global Alliance for the Rights of Nature. (2015). Rights for the Earth: Towards new international standards. https://www.endecocide.org/wp-content/uploads/2015/10/3-EarthLaws-DossierUPDATE.pdf

Global Alliance for the Rights of Nature. (2010). *Statutes of the Global Alliance for the Rights of Nature.* Adopted September 5, 2010, Hacienda Manteles, Patate, Ecuador. http://therightsofnature.org/founding-statutes/

Websites

Australian Earth Laws Alliance. (n.d.). *Home.* https://www.earthlaws.org.au/

Community Environmental Legal Defense Fund. (n.d.). *Rights of nature.* https://www.celdf.org/

Earth Law Alliance. (n.d.). *Home.* https://earthlawyers.org/

Earth Law Center. (n.d.). *Home.* https://www.earthlawcenter.org/

Gaia theory: Model and metaphor for the 21st century. (n.d.). https://gaiatheory.org/

Global Alliance for the Rights of Nature. (n.d.). *Home.* https://www.garn.org/

National Oceanic and Atmospheric Administration. (n.d.). *About our agency.* https://www.noaa.gov/about-our-agency

Pachamama Alliance. (n.d.). *Home.* https://www.pachamama.org/

Rights of mother earth. (n.d.). https://www.rightsofmotherearth.com/

Stop Ecocide International. (n.d.). *Home.* https://www.stopecocide.earth/

Index

www.ingramcontent.com/pod-product-compliance
Ingram Content Group UK Ltd.
Pitfield, Milton Keynes, MK11 3LW, UK
UKHW041827031026
15587UKWH00002B/617

9 783631 939130